"In *Walking with Mary*, Ted Sri achieves something rare and wonderful: a book that seamlessly combines rich biblical scholarship, a son's insight into the human heart of Mary, and an engaging, vividly accessible style the reader can't put down. This is a marvelous encounter with both the Word of God and the mother of Jesus Christ, the virgin of Nazareth, the model of all Christian discipleship."

—Charles J. Chaput, O.F.M. Cap., Archbishop of Philadelphia

"*Walking with Mary* is a highly readable book that illuminates the scriptural truth about Mary. Drawing on solid biblical scholarship and Catholic tradition, Dr. Sri leads his readers along the spiritual journey of the Mother of our Lord, from her initial call from God to her soul-piercing sorrow at the foot of the cross. With rich insight, he offers practical lessons for the personal challenges we all face as Mary's fellow pilgrims walking the path of faith. This book will help all Christians, not just Catholics, to get to know and love Mary much more."

—Dr. Scott Hahn, author of *The Lamb's Supper* and *Consuming the Word*

"A child of God has Christ for a brother—and Mary for a mother. This book delivers on the promise of its title. It's a long and lovely walk we take, on a glorious day, with Jesus and the mom he shares with us. This is what devotion was meant to be: living family life with God."

—Mike Aquilina, author of *Faith of Our Fathers: Why the Early Christians Still Matter and Always Will*

"This is no ordinary book! In it, Edward Sri combines a step-by-step Bible study on the life of the mother of Jesus with profound insights into the spiritual life of every Christian. The result is a biblical portrait of Mary of Nazareth that is both extremely informative and deeply moving. The sections on the sufferings of Mary alone are worth the price of the book. Must-reading for anyone who has ever wanted to know who the Virgin Mary really was and what her life means for us today."

—Dr. Brant Pitre, author of *Jesus and the Jewish Roots of the Eucharist*

Walking with Mary

A Biblical Journey from Nazareth to the Cross

EDWARD SRI

IMAGE
New York

Copyright © 2013, 2017 by Edward Sri

Published in the United States by Image, an imprint of the Crown Publishing Group, a
division of Penguin Random House LLC, New York.
crownpublishing.com

IMAGE is a registered trademark and the "I" colophon is a trademark of
Penguin Random House LLC.

Originally published in hardcover in the United States by Image,
an imprint of the Crown Publishing Group, a division of
Penguin Random House LLC, New York, in 2013.

Library of Congress Cataloging-in-Publication Data
Sri, Edward P.
Walking with Mary : a Biblical journey from Nazareth to the cross / Edward Sri. —
First Edition.
pages cm
1. Mary, Blessed Virgin, Saint—Biblical teaching. 2. Bible. New Testament—Criticism,
interpretation, etc. I. Title.
BT611.S65 2013
232.91—dc23
2013009201

ISBN 978-0-385-34805-8
Ebook ISBN 978-0-385-34804-1

Printed in the United States of America

Cover design by Nupoor Gordon
Cover photograph © DEA/A. Dagli Orti/Getty Images

10 9 8

First Paperback Edition

To my daughter Josephine

*With the divinest Word, the Virgin
Made pregnant, down the road
Comes walking, if you'll grant her
A room in your abode.*

— Saint John of the Cross[*]

* Saint John of the Cross, "Concerning the Divine Word," in *The Poems of St. John of the Cross,* trans. Roy Campbell (Glasgow: Collins-Fount Paperbacks, 1983), 89.

Contents

Acknowledgments

I express my gratitude to the many friends, colleagues, and students who have offered their prayers and encouragement throughout the writing of this book. I am thankful for the feedback and insights offered by Curtis Mitch, Jared Staudt, and Mark Giszczak and for my discussions with students at the Augustine Institute with whom I have explored Mary's journey of faith in various courses. I am particularly indebted to Paul Murray, O.P.—teacher, friend, and guide—for sharing with me throughout the years not only the epigraph for this book but also the many insights from the Catholic spiritual tradition that have found their way into the pages of this work. I thank Gary Jansen and the editorial team at Image Books for their suggestions that have helped make this a better book. I also thank my three oldest children, Madeleine, Paul, and Teresa, for our time opening the Scriptures together to study Mary's faith journey in the year of this book's production. Most of all, I am grateful for my wife, Elizabeth, for her prayers, support, and feedback and for her helping me find the time to make this work possible amid our full family life.

Introduction

"I'm not sure how devoted I've been to Mary. But I know she has been very devoted to me."

That's how a friend once described his relationship with the Blessed Virgin Mary. And his words capture an experience to which I can very much relate.

I grew up surrounded by Marian devotion in my home. Rosary beads by my mother's chair. Pictures of Our Lady and the holy child in my room. Hail Mary prayers at my bedside at night. Most of all, I will never forget those quick visits to a Polish Carmelite monastery just three blocks from my home in a town outside of Chicago. Almost every day my mother would stop by that monastery on our way back from school and take my siblings and me into a small, dark chapel with nothing to illuminate it but the dim refracted, colored light from the stained-glass windows and the rows of flickering red candles in front of the altars. For a child, walking into this mysterious chapel was like stepping into another world—into the realm of the sacred.

Our brief visits always culminated with the lighting of devotional candles and a prayer in front of a very large painting of Mary crowned in royal splendor with twelve stars on her head. Each child would have a candle lit for their intentions, and we would kneel down before this picture of Mary as my mother offered very personal, heartfelt prayers to the Lord. God was real. Prayer was real. And I knew Mary was an important person very close to God, and somehow (though I could not have explained it at the time) a profound part of my experience in prayer.

I would not want to give the impression that I had a particularly strong Marian devotion as I grew up and entered junior high and high school. But I did say my prayers, and thought of Mary from time to time, especially in moments when I was troubled. I suppose my relationship with Mary back then was similar to how many adult children relate to their own mothers: I love my mom. I sometimes take her for granted. I sometimes forget to call. But I know she's always there for me.

This youthful affection for Mary was severely shaken one night shortly after I went away to college.

On my dormitory floor at Indiana University, I met a joyful, outgoing Christian student named Rod. He called himself a "Bible Christian"—a term I had never encountered in my Chicago-area Catholic upbringing. But I figured that since I was Catholic and I also believed in the Bible, he and I would get along together quite well.

One night in the middle of the fall semester, however, I found out it would not be so easy. Rod came knocking on my door. He had a Bible in hand and a serious look on his face.

"Ted, can we talk?"

"Yes," I replied. "What's wrong?"

"Well, I'm worried about you."

"Why?"

"Because you're Catholic."

"Why are you worried about that?"

"Because if you're Catholic, I'm worried you'll go to hell."

I was utterly shocked. When I asked him why he thought my Catholicism would lead to my damnation, he said that Catholics believe so many things that go against the Scriptures. He proceeded to drill me with numerous pointed questions about Catholic beliefs and the Bible.

"Why do you Catholics confess your sins to a priest? Don't you know the Bible says only God can forgive our sins?"

"Why do you believe in purgatory? The word *purgatory* isn't even in the Bible!"

"Why do you believe in the pope? And why do you Catholics have all these man-made traditions? Don't you know that only the Bible is inspired by God?"

And then the questions about Mary came up.

"And why do you Catholics worship Mary? The Bible teaches that we're only supposed to worship God!"

"And why do Catholics pray to Mary? Don't you know we're only supposed to pray to God? All this worship of Mary is idolatry!"

I had no idea how to answer all these objections. At two a.m., after several hours of what felt like intense interrogation, my head was spinning. I went to bed confused and discouraged— and filled with many questions: *What does the Catholic Church really teach about these things? And is it really true?* Thankfully, some good books and some good Catholic friends showed me how the Church had been thinking about these issues for centuries, long before Rod came knocking on my door. I started studying the Bible more. And I began reading the writings of the early Christians and the teachings of the Catholic Church.

When it came to the subject of Mary, the more I studied, the more I realized how much the Scriptures actually support Catholic Marian doctrine. I also began to realize how many misconceptions there are about what Catholics believe about Mary. I came to see more clearly, for example, that Catholics don't worship Mary as we do the Holy Trinity, but we honor her, recognizing the great things God has accomplished in her life. And I came to appreciate how Catholics don't "pray to" Mary like they pray to God, but we ask her to intercede for us, just as Saint Paul exhorts all Christians to intercede for each other.

I am very thankful for Rod's difficult visit to my dorm room that evening long ago in Indiana, because it set me off on a quest to know and understand the Catholic faith of my childhood better, and it sparked a desire in me to pass it on to others. And that desire ultimately led me to pursue a doctorate in theology. As I look back now, I sense that Mary has, at least in some small but significant ways, been with me throughout this journey. I never set out to become a professor who would teach Mariology classes. But in my graduate studies I found myself developing a number of research papers on Mary and the Bible, and eventually I wrote a doctoral dissertation on this topic and have continued to publish articles and books expounding on the Marian texts in the Bible. Over time, biblical passages about Mary and their implications for Marian doctrine and devotion became one of the main topics for my study, prayer, and teaching.

But along the way I also have found myself drawn to learning more from Scripture about the person of Mary herself— the young woman of Nazareth who dwelt in Galilee some two thousand years ago and was called by God to a most extraordinary vocation. What would it have been like to have been Mary? What would the angel's message have meant to her? What might she have been going through during those early years of Jesus's childhood—experiencing the humble, poor conditions surrounding her son's birth, hearing Simeon's prophecy about a sword piercing her soul, and later on losing her child for three days and then finding him in the Temple? And what was God asking of Mary at those pivotal moments in Jesus's adult life—at his first miracle at Cana and at his death on the cross? Admittedly, the Bible does not offer a lot of detail about Mary's experience, but the sacred texts do provide some insights that can serve as windows, however small they might be, into Mary's soul and the particular spiritual path upon which the Lord was leading her.

In pondering Mary's journey of faith more, I have found new inspiration and encouragement for my own walk with the Lord and a desire to imitate her more in my life. That's why, even after many years of writing and teaching on Mary, in a sense I honestly feel I am only beginning to know her.

This book is the fruit of my personal journey of studying Mary through the Scriptures, from her initial calling in Nazareth to her painful experience at the cross. It is intended to be a highly readable, accessible work that draws on wisdom from the Catholic tradition, recent popes, and biblical scholars of a variety of perspectives and traditions. With the riches of these insights, we will ponder what her journey of faith may have been like in order to draw out spiritual lessons for our own walk with God. While there are many heroes and saints in the Bible who have qualities we can imitate, we will see that Mary stands out in Scripture as the first to say yes in the new covenant era and as a premier model of faith for us to follow. It is my hope, therefore, that whether you are of a Catholic, Protestant, or other faith background, this book may help you to know, understand, and love Mary more, and that it may inspire you to walk in her footsteps as a faithful disciple of the Lord in your own pilgrimage of faith.

Walking with Mary

Mary Walking with God

———— ❖ ————

I knew what my eleven-month-old daughter was thinking. Josephine stood by a chair holding herself up, contemplating her first step, but not sure she wanted to let go.

I was kneeling down only about five feet away with my arms open wide, ready to catch her if she fell. With a big smile on my face, I cheered her on. "Come on, Josephine! You can do it! Let go and come to Daddy!"

She smiled back, and I could tell she was ready to make the move. She let go, abandoning the security of the chair, and stood all on her own for the first time. Would she now take that risky first step?

"Come to Daddy, Josephine! You can do it!"

Suddenly her knees started to quiver. Her legs began to shake, and the look on her face changed from excitement to horror. In a panic she desperately reached back for the chair and caught her balance just in time. She clung on for dear life, wearing a sad look of fear as if to say, "No Dad. I don't think I want to try this."

But I egged her on and encouraged her to give it another shot. She eventually let go of the chair again, but this time, when her legs began to tremble, instead of going back to the chair she came wobbling toward me. She fell five steps forward and landed in my arms—her first steps! She laughed and crawled back to the chair to try it again. Seven steps on her second attempt. Back to the chair. We played this game for a long time that afternoon and she grew in confidence with each new step. Gradually she began walking for greater and greater distances, and within a few weeks crawling was just not as interesting. Walking became Josephine's primary mode of transportation.

Our Walk with God

We all have experienced moments in life when we have had to take a step toward something unknown. It could be moving to a new city, going through a job restructuring, or starting a new relationship. Walking into uncharted territory often comes with a bit of fear and trembling.

Similarly, although walking with God in faith can be a thrilling adventure, it also has some unsettling elements. If we truly allow him to guide our lives, we will be challenged to step out into the unknown, give up control, and rely more completely on him. And that is not something we easily do. But it may be comforting to know that while our Heavenly Father invites his people to follow him with ever greater levels of trust and surrender, he calls them to take only one step at a time.

We see this in biblical heroes like Abraham. God promised him many blessings and descendants, but Abraham first had to leave his home and move to a distant land, trusting that God would bless him there. Similarly, Moses had to take those first steps out of Egypt into a barren desert, unsure of what trials he would face as he led the Israelites toward the Promised Land.

We see this also in the saints throughout the Christian era. These holy men and women did not become saintly figures overnight. They all had to learn to walk with the Lord one step at a time. And at each step they were confronted with new opportunities to grow in love and service. Saint Anthony of the Desert was drawn to sell all his possessions and give his money to the poor. Saint Augustine was called to give up a quiet life of prayer and study to serve as a busy bishop administering church affairs and attending to his people's daily needs. St. Thérèse of Lisieux was inspired to seek out the people who hurt her and frustrated her the most and show them small acts of kindness.

Some of the saints were drawn to give up something they liked, move to a new place, or let go of something comfortable and familiar. God called Saint Francis Xavier, for example, to leave Europe and bring the Gospel to the Far East. He prompted the extroverted Saint Teresa of Avila to give up extra socializing in order to cultivate a deeper interior silence and union with him. At still other times, God drew the saints closer to him through intense trials and darkness, persecutions and misunderstandings. Saint John of the Cross was mistreated and imprisoned in a dark, cramped dungeon for nine months by his fellow Carmelites. But it was precisely through his being deprived of all worldly security and comfort that he gained a deeper mystical understanding of the spiritual life and experienced a profound encounter, in the very core of his being, with a God who lovingly pours himself out to fill our emptiness and gives inner strength to souls amid the darkness. Mother Teresa faced decades of painful spiritual darkness in which she did not sense God's closeness in her life, but eventually came to see that her feeling unwanted and forsaken allowed her to identify herself more with the loneliness and isolation of the poor and with Jesus himself who experienced suffering and rejection on Good Friday. Like a child learning to let go of the chair and walk, the saints gradually—through many ordeals—learned to abandon themselves ever more completely to God and walk in his ways.

The same is true for the Blessed Virgin Mary.

Christians may know Mary was an important woman in God's plan of salvation. After all, she was chosen to be the Mother of God's Son! And Catholics, in particular, have a special affection for Mary. They sing hymns dedicated to her, recite various Marian prayers, and celebrate special feast days in honor of Mary. Catholic churches are decorated with statues, pictures, icons, and stained-glass windows depicting her splendor. And Catholic theology teaches that she is the Immaculate Conception, the Ever-Virgin Mother of God, and the Queen of Heaven and Earth.

Mary's Humanness

We may know the Mary of sacred music, sacred art, and sacred theology—all of which beautifully express important aspects about the mystery of the mother of God—but how well do we know the *humanness* of Mary? How familiar are we with Mary's pilgrimage of faith and the important steps the Lord invited her to take throughout her life?

Mary was endowed with unique graces and privileges in Christ's kingdom, but she was still a woman who had her own faith journey to make—and one that we can relate to in many ways. She experienced the joys of parenthood and the blessings of following God's plan. But she also experienced the devastation of watching her son be misunderstood, rejected, and killed on the cross. Sometimes she was treated with dignity and honor. Other times she was humbled and oppressed. On some occasions God made his will clear for her, and she wholeheartedly committed herself to what the Lord was asking in that moment. But there were other times when it was not so apparent what the Lord was doing in her life and what she was supposed to do next.

When Mary was confronted with God's call at pivotal moments in her life, she chose to remain open to the Lord's plan for her every step of the way, even though what lay ahead for her was not always clear. Not everything was revealed to her all at once. There were moments when Mary did not understand what was happening and moments when she was not in control—moments when all she could do was prayerfully keep all these things and ponder them in her heart, awaiting God's fuller revelation to her (Luke 2:19, 51). Like all followers of Christ, Mary had to walk by faith, and not by sight.

A Continuous Fiat

New Testament scholar Francis Moloney emphasizes that Mary's faith was not completed at the Annunciation with her "fiat"—her "yes" to God's call for her to become the mother of the Messiah (Luke 1:38). Moloney explains that Mary's assent had to be repeated over and over again as she watched her son grow from a child into a man:

> Mary's *Fiat* did not lift her out of the necessary puzzlement, anxiety and pain which often arises [*sic*] from the radical nature of the Christian vocation. Despite her remarkable initiation into the Christian mystery, she still had to proceed through the rest of her life, "treasuring in her heart" the mysteries revealed to her, never fully understanding, but patiently waiting for God's time and God's ultimate answer.[*]

Blessed John Paul II sees Mary's "fiat" at the Annunciation as just the beginning of a profound spiritual trek. He describes it as "the point of departure from which her whole 'journey towards God' begins, her whole pilgrimage of faith." Mary will be required to exhibit total trust in God, which means "to abandon oneself" to the living God and the mystery of his will. Indeed, Mary's faith will be tested over and over again. And each time she will pass the test, "accepting fully and with a ready heart everything that is decreed in the divine plan."[†]

In this book we will walk with Mary on her journey of faith from the Annunciation to the cross to her sharing in Christ's heavenly reign. The Scriptures will be our guide and our primary point of departure. We will focus on nine pivotal moments in her walk with the Lord—nine steps in the journey of faith that God invites her to take as seen in the Scriptures.

---

[*]Francis Moloney, *Mary: Woman and Mother* (Eugene, Ore.: Wipf and Stock, 2009), 27.

[†]John Paul II, *Redemptoris Mater* (March 25, 1987), 14.

The nine steps I map out in this book are meant to be an instructive device to help take in many of the key moments in Mary's pilgrimage of faith. For simplicity, I focus on the Gospels of Luke and John—the two New Testament books in which Mary's role in the narrative stands out the most, and the Gospels that provide the most information about her.*

But before we begin walking with Mary, let's put ourselves in her shoes at the start of her pilgrimage of faith and consider what her life was like as a young woman, betrothed to Joseph, in the small village of Nazareth.

---

*If other New Testament texts were considered, attention could be drawn to other moments in Mary's life, such as the flight to Egypt (Matt. 2:13–15) or how Joseph's thinking about divorcing Mary might have affected her (Matt. 1:18–19).

In Her Shoes

The Original Mary

W hat was Mary's life like *before* the angel Gabriel appeared to her?

We don't know much for sure. Mary's early years are shrouded in mystery. Although various traditions have arisen, for example, about her birth to wealthy parents who struggled with sterility, her being raised as a child by the priests in the Temple, and her arranged betrothal to a widower named Joseph, the Bible doesn't tell us much about Mary's existence before the Annunciation. The Gospel of Luke offers only the following:

> In the sixth month the angel Gabriel was sent from God to
> a city of Galilee named Nazareth, to a virgin betrothed to a
> man whose name was Joseph, of the house of David; and the
> virgin's name was Mary. (Luke 1:26–27)

On Mary's early years, Luke doesn't give us much to work with. But he does offer three important facts we will explore:

She is living in "a city of Galilee named Nazareth." She is a virgin who is betrothed. The man to whom she is betrothed is named Joseph who is from the house of David.

These details may, at first glance, seem rather insignificant—background information that one can easily gloss over. When viewed in the context of Mary's first-century Jewish setting, however, these tiny facts reveal some important aspects about Mary's life that will be critical for understanding the mission God gives to her. And, as we will see, they give us at least a glimpse of Mary's life before the fateful day when the Holy Spirit overshadows her and she becomes the mother of the Messiah.

Nowhere Nazareth

The first fact we learn about Mary is that she dwelt in "a city of Galilee named Nazareth" (Luke 1:26). This small geographical detail is important because, from a human perspective, Nazareth of Galilee was a most unlikely place for the messianic era to begin.

Jews in Galilee were not always held in high esteem by their counterparts in Jerusalem and Judea (John 1:46; 7:52)—probably because of the many foreign people who had long dwelt in Galilee (cf. Matt. 4:15–16), and the region's distance from the holy city of Jerusalem. Nazareth was a small, secluded agricultural village in Galilee. Far from the social and religious center of the Jerusalem Temple, Nazareth had only about two hundred to five hundred inhabitants in Mary's day and was not located along any major trade route. Moreover, the village held no significance in the Jewish tradition. There are no prophecies explicitly about Nazareth, and the Old Testament never mentions the place.

The fact that Jesus comes from Nazareth will be a mark against him later in his public ministry, for the place did not seem to have a good reputation. Nathaniel's famous line, "Can anything good come out of Nazareth?" (John 1:46) illustrates how at least some Jews looked upon Nazareth with low regard. Therefore in the first-century Jewish world Nazareth of Galilee would not have made it onto most people's Top 10 list of the likely places from which the Messiah would come. That God chose a woman from *this* lowly city to become the mother of the Messiah would have been astonishing. It's especially remarkable in juxtaposition with what has recently happened to her kinsman Zechariah in Jerusalem.

In the previous scene recorded in Luke's Gospel, the angel Gabriel visits Zechariah when he is in a *sacred place*—the Temple in Israel's religious capital, Jerusalem. And Zechariah is a public figure holding a *sacred office,* serving as a Levitical priest. He is in the middle of performing a *sacred function* in the Temple liturgy when Gabriel appears to deliver the message that Zechariah's barren wife, Elizabeth, will conceive a child in her old age. Mary, in contrast, is an unknown young woman, holding no official position, and apparently going about her ordinary daily life in the insignificant village of Nazareth when the angel speaks to her.

Moreover, the annunciation to Zechariah has an immediate public impact, since the multitude of people gathered at the Temple perceive that their priest has had a vision (Luke 1:10, 21–22). Yet the angel speaks to Mary intimately with no one else around. Thus her revelation escapes the notice of everyone in all of Israel—even though this is the most important angelic announcement in all of history!

John Paul II pointed out how the contrast between these two announcements underscores the extraordinary nature of God's intervention in Mary's life:

> In the Virgin's case, God's action certainly seems surprising. Mary has no human claim to receiving the announcement of the Messiah's coming. She is not the high priest, official representative of the Hebrew religion, nor even a man, but a young woman without any influence in the society of her time. In addition, she is a native of Nazareth, a village which is never mentioned in the Old Testament.

By highlighting Mary's humble existence, John Paul II continues, "Luke stresses that everything in Mary derives from a sovereign grace. All that is granted to her is not due to any claim of merit, but only to God's free and gratuitous choice."* Mary thus stands in the biblical tradition of God choosing the people we'd least expect to play a crucial role in his plan of salvation. Just as God chose Moses, a man who was slow of speech and unconfident in his leadership abilities, to guide the people out of slavery in Egypt; and just as God chose from among all of Jesse's children the youngest boy named David, who was a simple shepherd and harpist, and made him Israel's next king; so God chooses from among all the people in first-century Judaism, not a woman from the Jewish aristocracy, nor the daughter

---

*John Paul II, General audience, May 8, 1996, in *Theotokos: Woman, Mother, Disciple* (Boston: Pauline Books, 2000), 88–89.

of a chief priest in Jerusalem, nor the wife of a famous law-yer, scribe, or Pharisee, but an unknown virgin named Mary from the lowly village of Nazareth and asks her to become the mother of Israel's long awaited Messiah-King.

Betrothed, Not Engaged

The second fact we learn about Mary is that she was "a vir-gin" who was "betrothed." This tells us three important things about Mary.

First, since Jewish women were typically betrothed around the age of thirteen, Mary probably was very young when she re-ceived this most weighty message from the angel Gabriel about her call to serve as the mother of the Messiah.

Second, as a betrothed woman, Mary was legally married to Joseph but still living with her own family. Jewish betrothal was not the same as our modern notion of engagement. In an-cient Judaism, marriage was a two-stage process. The first stage, known as betrothal, involved the man and woman exchanging consent before witnesses (cf. Mal. 2:14). After this the couple would be considered legally married to each other as husband and wife. Yet the wife typically would remain living with her own family apart from her husband for a period of time, up to a year at most. Then the second step of the marriage process took place, the "taking" home of the wife to the man's home. This is when the marriage would be consummated and the hus-band would begin supporting his wife. Therefore as a betrothed woman Mary would be between these two stages of marriage when Gabriel appeared to her. Mary already was Joseph's wife at this time, but she was not yet dwelling with him.

Third, according to Jewish marriage customs in Galilee, sexual relations normally would not take place until after the second stage of the marriage occurred. Thus, since Mary is a young betrothed woman, she is fittingly called a "virgin" (Luke 1:27).

The House of David

The most striking fact about Mary from these verses in Luke's Gospel is that she is betrothed "to a man whose name was Joseph, of the house of David" (1:27).

This has important implications for Mary. It tells us that Mary is not part of any ordinary family; she now belongs to a *royal* family.* Indeed, the phrase "house of David" was used in the Old Testament in reference to the royal descendants of David,† the most famous family in Israel's history. David's heirs ruled over the kingdom of Judah for several centuries. And God promised David that his family would have an everlasting dynasty and that his kingdom would never end.

The Davidic dynasty seemed to come to a tragic halt in 586 BC when Babylon invaded Jerusalem, destroyed the Temple, and carried the people off into slavery. At that time, many of the Davidic sons were killed, and no Davidic descendant sat on the throne for the next six hundred years as one foreign nation after another occupied the land and ruled over the Jews.

---

*Luke does not make Mary's own ancestry clear. Since Mary's relatives Zechariah and Elizabeth are Levites, some might suggest she may have been from the tribe of Levi. But since Jews often married within the same tribe, Mary's marriage to someone from the "house of David" may point to her having her own lineage from the house of David (see Rom. 1:3).

†See 1 Sam. 20:16; 1 Kings 12:19, 13:2; and 2 Chron. 23:3.

In this period the Davidic dynasty seemed to be dormant, and the people were waiting for a new son of David to restore the kingdom as their prophets had foretold.

The situation was similar in the days of Mary and Joseph, when the Romans were the latest foreign power to control the land. In the first-century Jewish world of Roman occupation, therefore, being a part of "the house of David" did not bring the privilege, honor, and authority it had in the days when the kings of Judah reigned in Jerusalem. Mary's husband may be "of the house of David," but he is not reigning as a prince in some Jerusalem palace. Instead he works as a humble carpenter, living a quiet, run-of-the-mill life in the secluded village of Nazareth.

Some may wonder how Jesus could be considered to be of David's line when Joseph is only his foster father. The virginal conception of Christ, however, in no way would diminish Joseph's fatherhood, since his legal paternity would have established Jesus as being in the line of Joseph's family heritage. Reflecting on the genealogy of Jesus in Luke 3, which speaks of Jesus as being "the son (as was supposed) of Joseph . . . the son of David," one commentator explains: "There is no inconsistency in Luke's mind between the account of the virgin birth and the naming of Joseph as one of the parents of Jesus. From the legal point of view, Joseph was the earthly father of Jesus, and there was no other way of reckoning his descent. There is no evidence that the compilers of the genealogies thought otherwise."*

---

*I. Howard Marshall, *The Gospel of Luke,* New International Greek Commentaries (Grand Rapids, Mich.: Eerdmans, 1978), 157.

So, on the surface, there does not appear to be anything extraordinary about Mary's life. She is a young woman. She is betrothed to a man from the house of David. She lives with her parents in the insignificant, small village of Nazareth in Galilee. Yet Luke's Gospel is about to provide one more detail about Mary that reveals how underneath what appears on the surface to be a simple, average life, God has been doing something extraordinary to prepare her for a most important mission.

STEP 1

An Open Heart

———————— ❋ ————————

Mary in Dialogue with God (Luke 1:28–29)

The angel Gabriel's opening words to Mary are truly re-markable: "Hail, full of grace, the Lord is with you!" (Luke 1:28). No one in all of biblical history had ever been addressed quite like that before. Although most Christians are familiar with these words, they often miss the profound meaning of this greeting. This is even true for Catholics who echo Gabriel's salutation every time they recite the prayer known as the Hail Mary.

But what if you were a young Jewish woman living in first-century Galilee and were encountering these sacred words for the very first time? What would this greeting have meant to *you*?

Let's put ourselves in Mary's shoes and imagine being confronted by these words. Gabriel says three amazing things to Mary in this opening verse of his message: she is called to "rejoice," she is addressed as "full of grace," and she is assured that the Lord is with her.

Rejoice!

Gabriel's initial word to Mary—*Hail,* or *chaire* in Greek—means much more than a simple "hello." The word literally means "rejoice."

It is true that the word *chaire* was a common Greek greeting and is used this way in Luke's Gospel in contexts involving persons who were Greek speakers. Hence some scholars see in Gabriel's opening word to Mary nothing more than an ordinary salutation.[*] But Mary dwells in the Jewish village of Nazareth. And Luke's Gospel never uses *chaire* in a Jewish milieu to express an ordinary salutation. Moreover, the angel is delivering the most important announcement in human history. It seems quite unlikely, therefore, that Luke intends nothing more than a simple "hello" when Gabriel utters his first word to Mary.

The angel's call for Mary to rejoice actually recalls the way "Daughter Zion" was addressed in the Old Testament. Daughter Zion was a poetic personification of the city of Jerusalem and came to be a symbol for the faithful remnant of God's people who are called to rejoice over the coming messianic age. In fact, in the Septuagint (the most ancient Greek translation of the Hebrew Scriptures), the imperative form of rejoice (*chaire*) is always used in a context related to Zion being invited to share in the future joy that will come when God rescues his people (Joel 2:21–23; Zeph. 3:14; Zech, 9:9; cf. Lam. 4:21).[†]

---

[*] See, for example, Raymond Brown, *The Birth of the Messiah* (New Haven, Conn.: Yale University Press, 1999), 321–25.

[†] Moreover, the threefold pattern of *chaire* + address + divine action as the cause of joy in Luke 1:28 is also found specifically in the only Old Testament passages where the imperative *chaire* is found—passages in which *chaire* clearly serves as more than a simple greeting, for these passages invite God's people to rejoice in God's saving action. See

The book of Zephaniah, for example, uses the command *chaire* to call on God's people to rejoice in the Lord, the King, who is coming in their midst to take away their judgment and free them from their enemies:

> *Sing aloud [chaire], O daughter of Zion;*
>   *shout, O Israel!*
> *Rejoice and exult with all your heart,*
>   *O daughter of Jerusalem!*
> *The Lord has taken away the judgments against you,*
>   *he has cast out your enemies.*
> *The King of Israel, the Lord, is in your midst;*
>   *you shall fear evil no more.* (Zeph. 3:14)

Note the parallels between Zephaniah's oracle and Gabriel's announcement to Mary: Zephaniah's prophecy involves an invitation to joy; Gabriel calls Mary to rejoice (Luke 1:28). Zephaniah mentions the Lord's presence ("the Lord is in your midst"); Gabriel tells Mary, "The Lord is with you" (Luke 1:28). Zephaniah instructs Zion to "fear evil no more"; similarly Gabriel assures Mary, "Do not be afraid" (Luke 1:30). Finally, Zephaniah promises God's saving intervention with the coming of the King of Israel. This is exactly what the angel Gabriel announces to Mary: the King of Israel is coming in the child she will bear (Luke 1:31–33).

Zechariah is another prophetic book that uses the com-

Joel Green, *The Gospel of Luke,* New International Commentary on the New Testament (Grand Rapids, Mich.: Eerdmans, 1997), 86–87; John Nolland, *Luke 1–9:20* (Dallas: Word Books, 1989), 49–50. In Lamentations 4:21, the command to rejoice is used ironically in a parody of this theme.

mand to rejoice (*chaire*) to direct God's people to rejoice over the king coming to Jerusalem. This king will bring "peace to the nations" and his dominion "to the ends of the earth":

> *Rejoice greatly, O daughter of Zion!*
> *Shout aloud, O daughter of Jerusalem!*
> *Behold, your king comes to you;*
> *triumphant and victorious is he.* (Zech. 9:9)

In this way, the prophets Zephaniah and Zechariah foretell that one day the Lord will come to his people and rescue them from their enemies. He will come as king and restore Israel's dominion. And on that day, God's faithful people—symbolized by the figure of Daughter Zion—will be called to rejoice (*chaire*).

For centuries the Jews awaited the fulfillment of these prophecies. They yearned for the day on which they would taste the *joy* of the messianic age. Now, finally, that day has arrived. The angel Gabriel appears to Mary to announce that the Lord, the King, is coming to his people to establish his kingdom (Luke 1:31–33, 35). And Gabriel begins this entire message to Mary bearing the same invitation to joy that we hear in the Daughter Zion prophecies of Zephaniah and Zechariah. Gabriel's initial word to Mary—*chaire*, Rejoice!—right away signals that the messianic era is dawning. The Lord, the King, is coming to rescue Israel. And Mary, as the first recipient of this good news, should rejoice. Like the figure of Daughter Zion in the prophecies, Mary is called to rejoice in the saving work God will accomplish.

"Full of Grace"

The second point that stands out in Gabriel's greeting is the way he addresses Mary. The angel does not call her by her personal name—he does not say "Hail, *Mary*, full of grace." He simply says to her, "Hail, full of grace."

As numerous Scripture scholars have pointed out, it is as if Mary is being given a new name: "full of grace."* And in the Bible that is significant. This is not a mere nickname. When someone receives a new name in Scripture, God is revealing something about the essence of the person and the mission to which he or she is called. Abram's name, for example, is changed to Abraham (meaning "father of a multitude") because he is called to become the great patriarch of Israel (Gen. 17). Likewise, Jesus changes the apostle Simon's name to Peter (meaning "rock") because he has become the rock upon which Christ would build his Church (Matt. 16).

Mary is addressed as "full of grace," her new title, which points to something about the mission that is being entrusted to her. As John Paul II noted, "full of grace" is "the name Mary possesses in the eyes of God." He continues:

> In Semitic usage, a name expresses the reality of the persons and things to which it refers. As a result, the title "full of grace" shows the deepest dimension of the young woman of Nazareth's personality: fashioned by grace and the object of divine favor to the point that she can be defined by this special predilection.†

---

*See Green, *The Gospel of Luke,* 87.
† John Paul II, General audience, May 8 and 15, 1996 , in *Theotokos,* 88, 90.

The new name given to Mary suggests that she is being singled out for some special purpose in God's plan of salvation. But what is the meaning of this unique name? No one else in all of Scripture is ever addressed this way! The Greek word here that is traditionally translated "full of grace" is *kecharitomene.* The term means "graced" and describes someone who has been and continues to be graced. The word expresses how Mary is especially favored by God, who has benevolently bestowed on her a fullness of grace, a fullness of God's life dwelling within her.*

Moreover, the word is in the perfect tense, which describes an action that began in the past and continues to have its effect in the present. Mary being addressed as *kecharitomene,* therefore, points to how God has already been working in Mary's life, preparing her for her mission, before Gabriel ever appeared to her. She already has been graced by God, and she continues to be graced in the present.

"The Lord Is with You!" (Luke 1:28)

Third, let us consider the angel's assurance, "The Lord is with you" (1:28). Throughout the Bible, these words of greeting were used to address men and women who were called by God for a special task, one that would have an impact on all of Israel. Their mission would require much generosity, many sacrifices,

---

*In Ephesians 1:5–8, this verb is associated with the saving, transforming power of grace that makes Christians adopted children of God who experience redemption and forgiveness of sins. Here in Luke 1:28 it appears in the passive tense, which underscores how Mary's special favor is based on God's activity in her life. Mary is the recipient of this unique grace.

and great trust—and that is why they were given the assurance that they would not have to face these trials alone: God would be with them, guiding, protecting, and strengthening them.

Some of the greatest leaders in Israel's history are greeted with this message. For example, when God appears to Jacob and confirms the covenant blessing entrusted to him, he says, "Behold, I am with you and will keep you wherever you go, and will bring you back to this land; for I will not leave you until I have done that of which I have spoken to you" (Gen. 28:15).

Similarly, when God calls Moses at the burning bush to lead the people out of Egypt, he says, "I will be with you" (Exod. 3:12). Before Joshua leads the people into battle in the Promised Land, God says, "I will be with you; I will not fail you or forsake you" (Josh. 1:5). When an angel calls Gideon to defend the people from a foreign invasion, he greets Gideon saying, "The Lord is with you" (Judg. 6:12). When God puts David at the head of an everlasting kingdom, God reminds David of his faithfulness to him, saying, "I have been with you wherever you went" (2 Sam. 7:9). And when God calls Jeremiah to be a prophet to the nations, he says, "Be not afraid of them, for I am with you to deliver you" (Jer. 1:8).

From Moses to Jeremiah, the pattern is clear: "The Lord is with you" signals that someone is being called to a great mission that will be difficult and demanding. And the future of Israel is largely dependent on how well that person plays his part. As one commentator explained, "In all these texts, the destiny of Israel is at stake. The person to whom the words are addressed is summoned by God to a high vocation, and entrusted with a momentous mission, and . . . the religious history of Israel (and therefore of the world) depended, at that moment, on his response to the call."* But the person is assured that they are not alone. God will be with them in their mission, helping them do what they could not do on their own.

Put yourself in the story and imagine what these words would have meant for Mary. The angel's greeting, "The Lord is with you," is signaling that something big is about to be asked of her. Indeed, she is being called to stand in the tradition of Israelite heroes like Moses, Joshua, David, and Jeremiah—people who suffered, sacrificed, and gave themselves radically for the Lord. She is now being called to a daunting mission that will involve many challenges and hardships, and the future of God's people will depend on how she responds.

No wonder the Bible tells us that Mary felt "greatly troubled" when she heard these words! And notice: Luke's Gospel tells us that Mary was not as much unsettled by the angel appearing to her as she was by the angel's *words*: "But she was greatly troubled *at the saying,* and considered in her mind what sort of *greeting* this might be" (Luke 1:29). This is quite different from Zechariah's anxiety in the previous scene in Luke's Gospel. Zechariah responds with fear at the mere appearance of the angel in the Temple (Luke 1:12). In contrast, Mary is troubled by the angel's *words* and ponders their implications for her life. She recognizes that something weighty is about to be asked of her. Like Moses, Gideon, and others who are called by the Lord in this way, Mary is probably wondering what this mission entails and if she is capable of fulfilling it.

---

*John McHugh, *The Mother of Jesus in the New Testament* (London: Darton, Longman and Todd, 1975), 49.

"Do Not Be Afraid"

In response to Mary's concern, Gabriel says to her, "Do not be afraid, Mary, for you have found favor with God" (Luke 1:30).

Have you ever sensed that God may want you to do something daunting or make a change in your life? When the Lord knocks on the door of our hearts, some of us might feel a little trepidation. You sense you are supposed to tell someone that you are sorry, but a part of you doesn't want to admit you were wrong. You feel drawn toward giving more of yourself to your kids, but you are hesitant to give up all the time and energy you spend advancing your career. Or maybe you sense you shouldn't be watching a certain show on TV or viewing a particular website, but you don't want to give it up. Or you think God wants you to share your faith a little more and defend Christian values, but you are afraid of what others might think of you.

The Bible reveals that fear is a typical human response to God's call in our lives. When we sense the Lord may be inviting us to do something new, face some challenge, or make a significant change, we can feel a little uneasy: What will this mean for me? How will it all work out? Do I really need to give this up? Can I do this? Like Mary, we might feel "greatly troubled" when we sense the Lord might be asking us to do something difficult or unfamiliar.

These initial emotions of fear should not control us or keep us from pursuing God's will. Just because we feel troubled about an unexpected situation, a new possibility, an intimidating challenge, or a sense that the Lord is demanding something difficult from us does not mean we should close the door on what is unfolding before us. We need to be like Mary, who continued to ponder the meaning of what the Lord wanted to show her. As Luke's Gospel tells us, Mary "considered in her mind what sort of greeting this might be" (Luke 1:29).

Benedict XVI explains how this response to the Lord's initial call for her life is exemplary. He notes how the Greek word Luke uses for *considered, dielogizeto,* is derived from the Greek root word meaning "dialogue." The term denotes an intense, extended reflection, and one that triggers a strong faith.[*] This indicates that even though Mary is troubled by what the angel's greeting might mean for her life, she does not turn away from the Lord's call. She remains an attentive listener to God's Word. As Benedict XVI explains, "Mary enters into an interior dialogue with the Word. She carries on an inner dialogue with the Word that has been given her; she speaks to it and lets it speak to her in order to fathom its meaning."[†] Mary thus responds like Samuel, who at the first promptings of God stirring in his heart, did not close the door to God's call, but humbly put his life at the Lord's disposal, saying, "Speak, for your servant hears" (cf. 1 Sam. 3:10).

Our Own Annunciations

At this very early stage of Gabriel's visit, Mary already faces an important, albeit subtle, choice. When, through the angel's

---

[*] See Carroll Stuhlmueller, "The Gospel According to Luke," in *Jerome Biblical Commentary,* vol. 2, ed. Raymond Brown et al. (Englewood Cliffs, NJ: Prentice Hall, 1968), 122.

[†] Joseph Ratzinger, "Hail, Full of Grace: Elements of Marian Piety according to the Bible," in Hans Urs von Balthasar and Joseph Cardinal Ratzinger, *Mary: The Church at the Source,* trans. Adrian Walker (San Francisco: Ignatius Press, 2005), 70.

greeting, God begins to show her that he is calling her to some formidable task, will she be truly open to this call? Or will she, in fear, close herself off to the new possibility, never seriously weighing it as a pathway for her life? Mary chooses to remain open. She takes God's initial message to heart and considers the meaning of the angel's greeting. She chooses to remain in dialogue with God's Word.

Though Mary was given a unique vocation, all of us, at one time or another, will be called by the Lord to do something we would rather evade. We will face our own "annunciations," and like Mary we will need to choose between being open to new directions in which the Lord may want to take us or closing ourselves off from these possibilities out of fear or a willful clinging to our own plans.

The twentieth-century Catholic writer Denise Levertov makes this point in her meditative poem on the Annunciation:

> *Aren't there annunciations*
> *of one sort or another*
> *in most lives?*
> *Some unwillingly*
> *undertake great destinies,*
> *enact them in sullen pride,*
> *uncomprehending.*
> *More often*
> *those moments*
> *when roads of light and storm*
> *open from darkness in a man or woman*
> *are turned away from*

*in dread, in a wave of weakness, in despair
and with relief.**

For most of us, when the Lord knocks on the door of our hearts prompting us to do something difficult—whether it be giving up something we like, making a moral change in our lives, taking on a difficult task, or moving to a new place—we are afraid to let him in. We find the demands of the Lord too much. We thus close the door on our own "annunciations" and turn away from the path on which he may want to lead us.

From the outside, our lives may go on looking the same as before. But inside something profound has changed—our willingness to open wide the doors of our hearts to Christ, to surrender our lives entirely to the Lord, and to follow him wherever he wishes to lead us. Pathways that are for our good and that serve God's purposes in the world are averted. As Levertov writes, "Ordinary lives continue. But the gates close, the pathway vanishes."

Mary's response, however, is exemplary. She is presented with a challenging vocation, yet she responds with great courage.

*Called to a destiny more momentous
Than any in all of Time,
She did not quail. . . .*

---

*Denise Levertov, "Annunciation," in *A Door in the Hive* (New York: New Directions, 1989), 86–87. I am grateful to Paul Murray, O.P., for introducing this poem to me. See Paul Murray, *The Hail Mary: On the Threshold of Grace* (Liguori, Missouri: Liguori, 2010), 26–29.

She did not cry, "I cannot, I am not worthy,"
nor, "I have not the strength" . . .
Bravest of all humans,
consent illumined her.
The room was filled with its light,
the lily glowed in it,
and the iridescent wings.
Consent,
courage unparalleled,
opened her utterly.

"You Have Found Favor with God" (Luke 1:30)

But before Mary gives her final consent, Gabriel assures her, "Do not be afraid, Mary, for you have found favor with God" (Luke 1:30).

A couple things stand out in these words. First, when Gabriel initially appears to Mary, he addresses her with the more formal, exalted title "full of grace" (1:28). Now, in an effort to reassure her, Gabriel speaks to Mary in a more personal way, calling her by her given name. He does not simply say, "Do not be afraid," as has been said to many other people in the Bible. He tenderly says her name, speaking to her more personally: "Do not be afraid, *Mary.*"

Second, Gabriel encourages her not to be afraid of what is about to be asked of her, because the same God who has endowed her with a unique privilege of grace (1:28) will continue to strengthen her in her mission, for as he now explains, she has "found favor with God" (1:30).

But what does it mean for Mary to "find favor with God"?

In the Scriptures, "to find favor" with someone can describe a higher ranking person bestowing kindness and favor upon an inferior and putting him in an important role of leadership. For example, when the patriarch Joseph serves as a slave under Potiphar in Egypt, Genesis tells us that Joseph "found favor" in Potiphar's sight, and was put in charge of all of Potiphar's household (Gen. 39:4–6).

The phrase "find favor *with God*" brings to mind the many people in the Old Testament who were specifically chosen by God for an important office or mission that would bring blessing to others, similar to the way Joseph is placed in a role of leadership by Potiphar. Noah, for example, is the first person in the Bible to be described this way. In the midst of a corrupt world, Noah is one man who "found favor" with God, and as a result he is protected from the flood and chosen to be the head of the renewed human family (Gen. 6:8). Abraham, the instrument God uses to bring blessings to the whole world, is depicted as having found favor with the Lord (Gen. 18:1–5). Moses also "found favor" with God and becomes the covenant mediator who helps to reconcile the sinful people with the Lord at Mount Sinai (Exod. 33:12–17).

In each of these cases, the one who finds favor with God is specifically chosen by the Lord for a particular mission in his saving plan. Therefore, when the angel tells Mary she has "found favor with God," he is reassuring her that she is being chosen by the Lord. As Mary is greatly troubled, pondering in her mind what is about to be asked of her, Gabriel tells her that she is being commissioned to carry out a great saving work for God's people—like Noah, Abraham, Moses, Gideon, and others. She, too, has "found favor with God."

The angel has yet to reveal the particulars of Mary's mission. At this point, all that Mary knows is that she is to rejoice because God is coming to save the people from their enemies. And she is going to play some special role in his saving plan. The Lord will be with her in this endeavor, and she has found favor with God. But what is her mission? That will be unveiled in the next three verses.

STEP 2

A Servant of the Lord

"Let It Be [Done] to Me According to Your Word" *(Luke 1:30–38)*

Mary's next step in her walk with the Lord reminds me of a simple prayer that is as intriguing and inspiring as it is terrifying:

> *O Lord, please help me to do what you want me to do,*
> *say what you want me to say,*
> *go where you want me to go,*
> *And give up what you want me to give up.*

Have you ever said a prayer like this? Have you ever told God that you want to do his will? It is a wonderful moment when souls begin to realize that God has a plan for their life and start to seek God's will for them, whether it be for big decisions or for the small choices they face each day—how they spend their time, how they spend their money, how they live their family life, how they live their moral life. A Christian might ask

God, "Please show me what I am supposed to do, Lord, and I will do it." Indeed, a prayer like this, when spoken with heartfelt sincerity, reflects the disposition Mary exemplifies in the first half of the Annunciation scene: a true openness to God's plan for her life.

But openness is only the first step. If we dare to offer such a prayer, we should be prepared that the Lord might actually take us up on it. And that, for many people, is the frightening part. There may be a part of us that sincerely wants to do whatever God wants with our lives. But there is another part of us that is afraid to give up control and surrender our lives to him. Yet, if we are to truly walk with the Lord, we should be ready to respond as Mary did in the second half of the Annunciation scene—not just with an openness to God's purposes, but with a servant's heart and a loving desire to actually pursue his plans, not our own. She said, "Behold, I am the handmaid of the Lord; let it be [done] to me according to your word" (Luke 1:38).

A Royal Son

To appreciate Mary's great surrender—her "let it be [done] to me according to your word"—we must first consider the specific mission God has in store for her. Let's consider step-by-step the angel Gabriel's gradual unveiling of the extraordinary call entrusted to Mary.

First, the angel informs Mary that she is to become a mother: "And behold, you will conceive in your womb and bear a son, and you shall call his name Jesus" (Luke 1:31).

This alone would be quite exciting. When any woman first

learns that she will have a child, it is a memorable occasion. But Mary is about to find out that she is not going to be any ordinary mother. The angel goes on to reveal that she will become the most important mother in the history of the world, for she will conceive the child who will bring the story of Israel and the entire human family to its climax. Her son will be the great Davidic king whom the prophets said would restore the kingdom to Israel and gather all nations back into covenant with God. Let's look more closely at what Gabriel actually says to Mary about her child.

> He will be great, and will be called the Son of the Most High; and the Lord God will give to him the throne of his father David; and he will reign over the house of Jacob forever; and of his kingdom there will be no end. (Luke 1:32–33)

These words would have been very familiar to many Jews in the first century, for they echo one of the most important Old Testament passages related to the Davidic kingdom. In 2 Samuel 7, God promises David an everlasting dynasty, saying:

> I will make for you a *great* name. . . . When your days are fulfilled and you lie down with your fathers, I will raise up your offspring after you, who shall come forth from your body, and I will establish his kingdom. He shall build a house for my name, and I will establish *the throne of his kingdom for ever. I will be his father, and he shall be my son. . . .* And your house and *your kingdom shall be made sure for ever*

before me; *your throne shall be established for ever.* (2 Sam. 7:9, 12–14, 16; emphasis added)

Notice the many striking parallels between what was promised to David in 2 Samuel 7 and what Gabriel says about Mary's child here in the first chapter of Luke. Just as David is told his name will be "great" (2 Sam. 7:9), so Mary is told her child will be "great" (Luke 1:32). Just as the descendants in David's dynasty are described as having a unique father-son relationship with God (2 Sam. 7:14), so Jesus "will be called Son of the Most High" (1:32). Just as God promises he will establish the throne of David's kingdom forever (2 Sam. 7:13), so will the Lord give Jesus "the throne of his father David" (Luke 1:32). And just as God tells David, "your house and your kingdom shall be made sure for ever" (2 Sam. 7:16), so Gabriel announces that Mary's child "will reign over the house of Jacob for ever; and of his kingdom there will be no end" (1:33).

2 Samuel 7	Luke 1
"I will make for you a great name" (7:9)	"He will be great" (1:32)
"I will be his father, and he shall be my son" (7:14)	"He . . . will be called Son of the Most High" (1:32)
"I will establish the throne of his kingdom forever" (7:13)	"And the Lord God will give to him the throne of his father David" (1:32)
"And your house and your kingdom shall be made sure forever" (7:16)	"And he will reign over the house of Jacob for ever, and of his kingdom there will be no end" (1:33)

Thus, Gabriel's description of Mary's child is shouting out with the promises God made to David's dynasty. By harkening back to the Davidic themes of greatness, sonship, throne, house, and an everlasting kingdom, Gabriel is highlighting that Mary will bear the ultimate royal son of David who will fulfill the promises to David about the everlasting kingdom. The Jews called this long-awaited child the "anointed one"—or in Hebrew, the *Messiah*.

Mother of the Son of God

As profound as this messianic message would have been for Mary, it pales in comparison to what happens next. Mary asks how she, as a virgin, can have a child since she does not know man (Luke 1:34). In response, Gabriel provides a fuller picture of just how extraordinary this conception will be and how important the child is whom she will bear:

> *The Holy Spirit will come upon you,*
> *and the power of the Most High will overshadow you;*
> *therefore the child to be born will be called holy,*
> *the Son of God.* (Luke 1:35)

These words reveal the divine origins of this child. Mary learns that she will not conceive this child through natural sexual relations, but by the Holy Spirit. There had never been a conception like that before! And to top it all off, Gabriel tells Mary that her child will be called "Son of God"—not merely in reference to his function as the Messiah, for the Davidic kings are described figuratively as God's sons (see 2 Sam. 7:14). Even more fundamentally, Mary's child here is called the Son of God in connection with his conception by the Holy Spirit.*

What Was Mary Thinking?

We don't know what Mary was thinking when she heard all this from Gabriel. But put yourself in her shoes. In the midst of her ordinary day, an angel suddenly appears. That alone would be quite startling. Next, this angel greets her, saying, "The Lord is with you" and "you have found favor with God"—two Old Testament expressions that signal that Mary is being called to an important and difficult mission on behalf of God's people. Then, the angel tells her that she will have a child and that this child will be the long-awaited Messiah-King, the one who would fulfill all the prophecies about the Davidic kingdom. And if that's not enough, Gabriel also informs her that she will conceive this child in a way that has never occurred before—not by sexual relations, but by the power of the Holy Spirit. Finally, on top of all this, Gabriel announces that her child will just happen to be the Son of God.

That's an awful lot to take in from one short conversation with an angel! The only hint we receive about what Mary was experiencing in those pivotal moments before the Incarnation

---

*"Luke grounds this sonship not in Jesus's role but in his *origin*. Luke seems to be consciously opposing the view that Jesus's divine sonship is merely 'functional'—a special relationship with God by virtue of his role as king. He is rather the Son of God from the point of conception, before he has taken on any of the functions of kingship" (Mark Strauss, *The Davidic Messiah in Luke-Acts: The Promise and Its Fulfillment in Lukan Christology* [*Journal for the Study of the New Testament*, Supp. 110] [Sheffield, UK: Sheffield Academic Press, 1995], 93–94).

is her response: "Behold, I am the handmaid of the Lord; let it be to me according to your word" (Luke 1:38).

"The Handmaid of the Lord": A Lesson in Freedom

Mary's response to Gabriel's message is unique in all of biblical history. In other birth announcement scenes and commissioning scenes from the Old Testament, God or his heavenly messenger typically speaks last before departing. Abraham, Sarah, Zechariah, and Samson's parents, for example, do not give a grand statement of consent—a "fiat"—after receiving the announcements about their sons. And neither does Moses or Gideon when God commissions them for their great undertakings. Mary stands out for getting in the last word in the dialogue with the angel.* And the words of consent reveal much about Mary's desire to serve God:

> I am the handmaid of the Lord; let it be [done] to me according to your word. (Luke 1:38)

First, Mary describes herself as someone who has completely surrendered her freedom. The Greek word here translated as "handmaid," *doulē*, actually refers to a servant or slave—someone who is completely at the disposal of another.† The term is used in the New Testament to describe those who

---

*"The final word is always given to the supernatural voice" (Nolland, *Luke 1–9:20*, 57). See also Green, *The Gospel of Luke*, 93; and the table in Brown, *Birth of the Messiah*, 156.

† See Beverly Gaventa, *Mary: Glimpses of the Mother of Jesus* (Columbia: University of South Carolina Press, 1996), 54.

accept God's authority in their lives and serve his purposes (Acts 2:18; 4:29; 16:17). Even the apostle Paul speaks of himself as a slave of Christ (Rom. 1:1; Phil. 1:1; Gal. 1:10) and a slave of God (Titus 1:1).

This is the metaphor Mary uses to describe herself. She seeks to be a *doulē*—a servant—of the Lord, completely dedicated to fulfilling God's wishes. She has heard from the angel all that the Lord has planned for her, and she responds by placing her entire life at God's disposal. She has not sought out this mission for herself, but finds herself chosen and consents. As a servant of the Lord, she chooses to use her life not for her own purposes, but for God's.*

Francis Moloney notes that at the heart of Mary's self-identification as a servant is her surrendering of control over her life and her giving herself entirely to the Lord's plan:

> Now Mary is aware that she has been caught up into a plan of God that reaches outside all human measurement and control. She is being asked to give herself and her future history to "the Holy Spirit . . . the power of the Most High." She *could* have remained in the realm of the controllable, and baulked at such a suggestion. Instead she commits herself to the ways of God in a consummate act of faith (v. 38). . . . Her acceptance of that consummate vocation makes her—in Luke's story line—the first person to risk everything for the sake of Jesus Christ: the first of all believers.†

---

*"Instead of claiming herself for her own ends and purposes, she allowed the Lord to claim her for the kingdom of God" (Eugene LaVerdiere, *The Annunciation to Mary: A Story of Faith, Luke 1:26–38* [Chicago: Liturgy Training Publications, 2004]), 147.

† Moloney, *Mary: Woman and Mother*, 22–23.

This is a key insight into Mary's soul. There are many of us who want to serve God with our lives, but only on our own terms. We set up all sorts of limits, parameters, and conditions for where we will allow God to lead us. We *say* we are willing to do the Lord's will, but in reality a large part of us wants to make sure we can still pursue certain dreams and desires while avoiding what may be scary or demanding. We want to remain in the realm of control.

Mary surrendered that control. She placed her life completely at God's disposal. She was willing to do whatever the Lord might want her to do and go wherever he might lead her. She viewed human freedom not as something to be grasped at, something to be used just for her own purposes, but as a gift to give back to God and to be used for *his* plan. She thus freely chose to surrender control over her life and live as a servant—a *doulē*—of the Lord, trusting totally in his plan for her. In other words, she freely chose to limit her freedom and live completely dedicated to God's will. She lives her life as a total gift to God.

Archbishop Fulton Sheen once described Mary's gift of self as "the freedom of total abandonment to God." He wrote, "Our free will is the only thing that is really our own. Our health, our wealth, our power—all these God can take from us. But our freedom he leaves to us. . . . Because freedom is our own, it is the only perfect gift that we can make to God."* And when we offer our freedom back to God as a gift—when we live as servants of the Lord like Mary did—our lives are not deprived, but much enriched. Left to our own navigation, we tend to

*Fulton Sheen, *The World's First Love: Mary, Mother of God* (Garden City, NY: Garden City Books, 1952), 22.

make decisions based on a limited vision of life. We pursue our fallen, disordered desires. We are enslaved by a hundred fears, insecurities, and weaknesses. Yet we think we are free and in control of our lives.

It is only by learning to give up our freedom to do whatever *we,* in our fallen human nature, want, and by entrusting our lives entirely to a God who knows what is truly best for us and desires our happiness that we discover the deeper freedom to live life to the fullest—a freedom that is possessed only when we live totally in the Lord's plan.

Do with Me Whatever You Wish

If we sincerely tell God that we will pursue his plans for our lives—if we tell him that we will do whatever he wants—we should not be surprised if he takes us up on that offer from time to time, whether it be through certain circumstances he allows to unfold in our lives, surprising doors that suddenly open up, unexpected trials that come our way, or simply a profound sense that the Lord wants us to do something different, make a change, or give something up.

One modern woman who experienced an unexpected call in a most extraordinary way was Blessed Mother Teresa. Early in her life she gave herself to the Lord in a generous way, leaving her home in Albania to become a religious sister with a missionary order in India, taking vows of poverty, chastity, and obedience. Spurred on by her love for Jesus, she joyfully pursued this initial call and was very happy teaching at a school in Calcutta and living with her religious community, the Sisters of Loreto. But one day in 1946, while she was on a train ride en route to a retreat, she heard the voice of Jesus in her soul ask her to take yet another leap of faith and surrender. Jesus called her to leave her teaching position and to start a new religious community specifically dedicated to serving the poorest of the poor. She was, understandably, nervous about this new direction for her life and hoping Jesus would choose someone else.

But Jesus did not back away from his demands. Indeed, he pressed the matter further. While acknowledging that she had already given up a lot to follow him, he still firmly challenged her to take one more step in her journey of faith:

> You have become my Spouse for my Love—you have come to India for Me. The thirst you had for souls brought you so far. Are you afraid to take one more step for your Spouse— for me—for souls? Is your generosity grown cold—am I a second to you?[*]

Jesus then reminded her of the promise she had made to him—a prayer that many Christians have made in one form or another. He reminded her that she had said she would always do his will: "You have been always saying 'do with me what ever you wish," Jesus said to her. "Now I want to act—let me do it. . . . Refuse me not—Trust me lovingly—trust me blindly."[†]

If we are to be like Mary, a servant of the Lord, it is not enough to be open to God's will. We must be willing to let Jesus act. In the end, that is what Mother Teresa did. When she came to realize that it was truly Jesus's desire for her to leave her

---

[*] Mother Teresa, *Come Be My Light*, edited and with commentary by Brian Kolodiej-chuk (New York: Doubleday, 2007), 48.

[†] Ibid., 49.

past behind and start a new order, the Missionaries of Charity, she enthusiastically committed herself to this new direction, no matter what the cost might be for her.

Like the Blessed Virgin Mary, Mother Teresa viewed herself as a servant of the Lord. Like Mary, she surrendered her life to God's plan, and at the critical moments when the Lord made his will clear to her, she abandoned her own vision for her life in order to follow wherever the Lord was leading—which, in the end, is the only path to that abundant life God has in store for all of us.

Mary's Fiat

Mary's next words provide a window into her servant's heart and reveal the *manner* in which she pursued God's call for her: "Let it be [done] to me according to your word" (Luke 1:38). These words highlight how Mary *joyfully* seeks to serve the Lord. She does not view serving the Lord as a burdensome duty, a spiritual chore she is forced to do. She enthusiastically seeks to make her life a gift to God.

John Paul II and Scripture commentators have pointed out how Mary's "let it be [done] to me" (*genoito* in Greek) indicates not a passive acceptance of God's will, but an active, loving embrace of it. The particular mood of the word implies "a joyous desire to" serve God, not just a submission or acceptance of something difficult. As Scripture scholar Ignace de la Potterie explains, the expression of Mary is, in a sense, different from the "Thy will be done" of the Our Father and Jesus's prayer in Gethsemane:

The resonance of Mary's "fiat" at the moment of the Annunciation is not that of the "*fiat voluntas tua*" [thy will be done] of Jesus in Gethsemane, nor that of a formula corresponding to the Our Father. Here there is a remarkable detail, which has only been noticed in recent years, and which even today is frequently lost from sight. The "fiat" of Mary is not just a simple acceptance or even less, a resignation. It is rather a joyous desire to collaborate with what God foresees for her. It is the joy of total abandonment to the good will of God. Thus the joy of this ending responds to the invitation to joy at the beginning.[*]

Mary does not just submit to God's plan; she *longs* to fulfill it, "making it her own."[†] She responds like a lover who, once she sees what is on her Beloved's heart, enthusiastically and ardently seeks to fulfill his desires. She thus serves the Lord not merely out of duty. She is motivated by love.

---

[*] Ignace de la Potterie, *Mary in the Mystery of the Covenant* (New York: Alba House, 1992), 35.

[†] John Paul II, General audience, September 4, 1996, in *Theotokos*, 135.

Magnify the Lord

———————— ❈ ————————

The Humility of Mary (Luke 1:39–55)

How do you feel when you have a lot on your plate? I know when I have much to do, I can be tempted to close in on myself—focusing on my projects, my problems, my concerns—and not be as attentive to those around me. But Mary was not like that.

The next passage from Luke's Gospel—a scene known as the Visitation—reveals that in spite of all that has been entrusted to her, Mary does not turn in on herself. She remains focused on God and on other people. After hearing the angel's message, Mary goes "in haste" to the hill country of Judea to bring joy to her kinswoman Elizabeth who is pregnant with John the Baptist and to share with her all that God is accomplishing in Israel and in her own life. The one who received the angel's message of the Messiah's coming now becomes the first human messenger of the Good News.

The Meaning of the Sign

At the end of the Annunciation scene, the angel Gabriel gives Mary a sign—even though she did not ask for one. He informs her of her elderly kinswoman Elizabeth's miraculous pregnancy. Elizabeth, who was barren, has conceived a child in her old age. Mary would not have known about this since Elizabeth has been in seclusion for five months (1:24, 26).

This sign is meant to assure Mary. The same God who has accomplished in the elderly Elizabeth what seemed humanly impossible can work an even greater miracle in Mary's life, causing her to conceive even though she does not know man. Gabriel explains, "For with God nothing will be impossible" (1:37).

After hearing this news, Mary "arose and went with haste into the hill country, to a city of Judah" to visit Elizabeth (Luke 1:39). This would not have been a leisurely weekend trip. The roughly eighty-mile journey from Nazareth to the hill country of Judah would have taken about three to four days on foot, and usually a trek like this would be undertaken only in the company of traveling companions.

What is the purpose of Mary's visit? When Luke narrates this scene, he uses three small words in the opening sentence to indicate that Mary is not embarking on a simple vacation to see a relative. Mary's travel to the hill country of Judah is not just a journey on foot. It is meant to be understood as a *spiritual* journey.

First, Luke informs us that Mary *arose* and went to visit Elizabeth. The Greek word for *arose, anesteimi,* means more than "get up." It is used metaphorically here to describe the beginning of a new action. Elsewhere in Luke the word describes actions that imply great spiritual effort. The prodigal son, for example, "arose" and returned to his father, who welcomed him with a great feast (Luke 15:18, 20). Similarly, Levi the tax collector, in response to Christ's call, left everything and "rose" (*anastasa*) to follow Jesus (Luke 5:27–28).* So, too, Mary, after hearing from the angel the Lord's call in her own life, "arose" and began her journey to visit Elizabeth. Like the son in the parable and Levi the tax collector, Mary is embarking on a new journey with the Lord as she assumes her new mission as the mother of the Messiah.

Second, Mary arose and *went* to the hill country of Judah. Here Luke uses a key word that has rich theological meaning in his narrative. Though the Greek word for *went, poreuomai,* itself means "to go or to walk," Luke uses it elsewhere to describe a journey with a divine purpose, most notably Christ's journey from Galilee to Judea, where his messianic mission is fulfilled (Luke 9:51; 13:22; etc.).† Carrying the baby Jesus in her womb, Mary anticipates her son's climactic journey from Galilee to Judea by making her own trek from Nazareth of Galilee to the hill country of Judea (Luke 1:39), where she will proclaim the great works of the Lord.

Why the Hurry?

Next Luke informs us that Mary makes this journey "in haste," *meta spoudēs.* This phrase has been understood in varying ways.

---

* See John Paul II, General audience, October 2, 1996, in *Theotokos,* 139–40.

† Francois Bovon, *Luke* (Minneapolis: Fortress Press, 2002), 57–58; Arthur Just, *Luke 1:1–9:50* (St. Louis: Concordia Publishing House, 1996), 72; Cologero Milazzo, *Israele, Maria, la Chiesa* (Rome: Città Nova, 2010), 29–30.

Some have interpreted this haste as pointing to Mary's prompt obedience to the angel's message about Elizabeth's miraculous motherhood. Others have viewed it as pointing to Mary's desire to help her elderly kinswoman in the last trimester of her pregnancy or her eagerness to share with Elizabeth the special message she received from the angel.

These elements may be in the background, but it is worth noting that the particular phrase "in haste" also can be translated as "with thoughtfulness" or "with eagerness,"* which may get more to the heart of the matter. In this perspective, Mary's going in haste points to her joy and wonder over what God is accomplishing in Israel and in her own life by sending the Messiah-King. And this is a divine plan in which she and Elizabeth are now intimately bound through their experience of miraculous motherhood and the children they bear. Mary, thus, enthusiastically sets off to see the sign that Gabriel has given her about Elizabeth's pregnancy.

This is similar to the shepherds' response to the sign the angel gave them about the Christ child lying in the manger (Luke 2:12). Upon hearing of the sign, the shepherds enthusiastically "went with haste" to encounter the good news of salvation announced to them by the angel. They do not go to check if the angel was right. Neither do they receive a command from the angel to do this. Rather, on their own initiative, the shepherds eagerly desire to see what has been revealed to them by the angel. Mary likewise believes the angel's message and goes urgently to witness firsthand the great things God is

---

* Bovon, *Luke,* 58; John Nolland, *Luke 1.1–9:51,* 65; 3 Macc. 5:24; Blaise Hospodar, "*Meta spoudēs* in Luke 1:39," *Catholic Biblical Quarterly* 18 (Jan. 1956), 14–18.

doing in Elizabeth's life. As one theologian explained, Mary's haste "sprang from the joy of her vocation and from the hope that welled up in her. Mary, joyful, hopeful and ready, went in search of the signs from God."[*]

An Extraordinary Greeting

The fact that Mary arrives at Elizabeth's house and greets her is exactly what we would expect. By first-century Jewish standards, Elizabeth is clearly the superior. Elizabeth is the elder of the two. Moreover, she has honorable family ties as a descendant of Israel's first high priest, Aaron, and as the wife of a priest named Zechariah (Luke 1:5). It was customary for the younger to greet the elder and those with lower status to greet those in higher positions of honor (see Exod. 18:7; Luke 7:36–50, 20:46). So by greeting Elizabeth, Mary is doing what would be expected of a good Jewish woman.

What is remarkable is the way Elizabeth goes on to greet Mary. Prompted by the baby leaping in her womb, Elizabeth bestows on Mary extraordinary accolades that reveal Mary to be one of the most important people in the Bible whom God would involve in his plan of salvation.

> She exclaimed with a loud cry, "Blessed are you among women, and blessed is the fruit of your womb! And why is this granted me, that the mother of my Lord should come to me?" (Luke 1:42)

---

[*] Joseph Paredes, *Mary and the Kingdom of God: A Synthesis of Mariology* (Middlegreen, UK: St. Paul Publications, 1991), 47.

All this comes out of Elizabeth's mouth before Mary has the chance to say a word about the angel's visit in Nazareth and her own miraculous pregnancy. So how does Elizabeth know Mary is bearing a child in her womb? And how does she know Mary is not the mother of any ordinary child but "the mother of my Lord"? Mary certainly didn't send Elizabeth a letter or a text message ("Im preg 2!") or change her status on Facebook ("Betrothed, but pregnant"). So how did Elizabeth know?

Luke's Gospel gives one clue that sheds light on how Elizabeth had this insider knowledge. Luke notes that when Elizabeth uttered these words, she was "filled with the Holy Spirit"; phrases like this elsewhere in the Bible are used to describe a person who is given prophetic insight.* Thus, it is through the prompting of the Holy Spirit that Elizabeth praises Mary for her unique pregnancy, hailing her as "blessed among women," as "the mother of my Lord," and as "she who believed that there would be a fulfillment of what was spoken to her from the Lord" (Luke 1:42–45).

Blessed Among Women

Let's consider the meaning of each of these three accolades. First, Elizabeth says to Mary, "Blessed are you among women" (Luke 1:42). These words bring to mind how two heroines of the Old Testament, Jael and Judith, are described. They are the only other women in all of Scripture who have been given such praise.

After Jael defeated a pagan general who was oppressing

---

*See Luke 1:41; 1 Sam. 10:10; 2 Sam. 23:2; Ezek. 11:5; 2 Kings 2:9–16.

God's people, the prophetess Deborah proclaimed, "Most blessed of women be Jael" (Judg. 5:24). Similarly, when Judith defeated a pagan commander who was attempting to overtake a Jewish town, Uzziah said to her, "O daughter, you are blessed by the Most High God above all women on earth" (Jth. 13:18). Both Jael and Judith, therefore, were considered blessed among women because the Lord used them to rescue the people from their enemies.

Mary stands in this tradition as she is called "blessed among women." Like Jael and Judith, Mary also is instrumental in God's plan for rescuing Israel. But there is one crucial difference. Unlike these warrior women of old, Mary is not engaging in a physical battle. She is participating in God's saving plan for Israel through bearing Jesus in her womb. This is precisely what Elizabeth goes on to explain to her. She says to Mary that she is blessed among women because "blessed is the fruit of your womb" (Luke 1:42). Mary is blessed because the child she bears is the one who will accomplish God's plan of salvation for Israel. And, as Luke's Gospel makes clear, the kind of salvation this child brings involves a lot more than the political liberation Jael and Judith helped to bring about. The child in Mary's womb is coming to save his people from a much darker enemy: sin.

Mary also shares with Jael and Judith a common association with the imagery from Genesis 3:15. Jael and Judith are blessed among women because they struck the heads of their enemies. This recalls the imagery foreshadowing the future Messiah given in Genesis 3:15,* where God foretells that the

---

*See *Catechism of the Catholic Church* (Rome: Urbi et Orbi Communications, 1994), para. 410.

woman would have a son who would crush the head of the serpent, the devil. Jael's and Judith's defeats of Israel's military enemies by striking their leader's heads can be seen as anticipating the one who will crush the head of Israel's greatest enemy, the devil. Mary is associated with the ultimate fulfillment of Genesis 3:15. She is the "woman" whose son brings about the defeat of the devil as Genesis 3:15 foreshadows (Rev. 12:1–9; cf. John 2:4, 19:25–27).

"The Mother of My Lord"

Next, Elizabeth addresses Mary as "the Mother of my Lord." In doing so Elizabeth hails Mary as the mother of the King. In the Old Testament "my Lord" was a court expression used to honor the king (see 2 Sam. 24:21; Ps. 110:1). Thus, Elizabeth is referring to Mary as the mother of the King.

For Mary, Elizabeth's words are a confirmation of what the angel told her in Nazareth. She is the mother of the Davidic king. But Elizabeth's words also confer quite a significant honor on Mary herself, for in the biblical world, as mother of the King, Mary would have been understood to be the queen in her son's kingdom.*

In ancient Israel the queenship in the Davidic kingdom was bestowed not on the king's wife but on the king's mother (see Jer. 13:18, 20; 1 Kings 15:13; 2 Kings 24:15; cf. 1 Kings 2:19–20). Most kings had large harems with many wives, but each king had only one mother, and the queenship was given to her.

---

*See Edward Sri, *Queen Mother: A Biblical Theology of Mary's Queenship* (Steubenville, Ohio: Emmaus Road Publishing, 2005).

Therefore, when Elizabeth calls Mary "Mother of my Lord," she is honoring Mary as the mother of the King, the queen mother.

This background can shed some biblical light on Mary's intercessory role today, for the queen mother in ancient Israel served as an advocate for the people. Members of the kingdom would bring petitions to the queen mother and she would present those requests to the king (see 1 Kings 2:13–20). If Mary is the mother of King Jesus, the queen mother in Christ's kingdom, then it would make sense that she serves as an advocate for the citizens of the kingdom, bringing our petitions to her royal Son.

"Blessed Is She Who Believed"

Finally, Elizabeth praises Mary for her great faith: "Blessed is she who believed that there would be a fulfillment of what was spoken to her from the Lord" (Luke 1:45). Notice the difference in this third acclamation. In the first two accolades, Elizabeth honors Mary for her unique maternity, recognizing Mary is blessed because of the fruit of her womb and because she is the "mother of my Lord." But in this third statement Elizabeth exalts Mary for something even greater: her faith: "Blessed is she who believed."

Saint Augustine explained that although being the mother of the Savior bestows on Mary a great privilege, her faithfulness is something even more noteworthy. Even more than the physical relationship she has with her son, Mary's spiritual walk with the Lord as a disciple is what makes her most blessed. Augustine wrote, "We must not think that blessedness lay in bodily relationship"; instead, he concluded, "Mary is blessed because she 'heard the word of God and kept it' [Luke 11:28]."

> Indeed and indeed she did the Father's will and it is a greater thing for her that she was Christ's disciple than that she was his mother. It is a happier thing to be his disciple than to be his mother. Blessed then is Mary who bore her Lord in her body before she gave him birth.*

A Soul that Magnifies God

It's hard to imagine Mary receiving any greater words of praise. She is blessed among women because of the child she carries, the blessed fruit of her womb. She also is "the mother of my Lord." Most of all, she is blessed for her belief. How does Mary respond to all these accolades? With humility. She turns all the attention back to God, recognizing him as the true source of all these blessings in her life. She says, "My soul magnifies the Lord, and my spirit rejoices in God my Savior" (Luke 1:46–47).

Here we turn to the climactic part of the Visitation scene, where Mary's hymn-like response to Elizabeth's praise sheds additional light on Mary's interior life. The verses of Luke 1:46–55 are commonly known as the Magnificat, a title taken from the Latin translation of Mary's first words in these verses: *Magnificat anima mea Dominum* (My soul *magnifies* the Lord). The word *magnify*, in Greek *megalunein*, means "to make great,

---

*Augustine, Sermon 25, 7–8, in *Nuova Biblioteca Agostiniana* 30 (1983), 468–79 (as translated in Moloney, *Mary: Woman and Mother*, 28).

to extol or praise."* When Mary says that her soul magnifies the Lord, she is expressing how in the very depths of her being, she desires to praise God, to make God great.

Do you desire to praise God, to make God great, in your soul? If so, Mary exemplifies how to do that in the Magnificat. The first half of her song reveals that Mary's soul magnifies God because of her humility.

> *And Mary said,*
> *"My soul magnifies the Lord,*
> *and my spirit rejoices in God my Savior*
> *for he has regarded the low estate of his handmaiden.*†
> *For behold, henceforth all generations will call me blessed;*
> *for he who is mighty has done great things for me,*
> *and holy is his name.*
> *And his mercy is on those who fear him*
> *from generation to generation.* (Luke 1:46–50)

Humility involves seeing the truth about one's self, and Mary exhibits this virtue in notable ways in the Magnificat. First, she acknowledges the truth about the unique mission entrusted to her and the extraordinary blessings she has received. Mary does not deny or downplay what the Lord has accomplished in her life. God has, indeed, done great things for her, she says. And all generations will call her blessed.

---

*The verb *megalunein* is used in the Psalms to describe praise of God (see Ps. 34:3, 40:16, 69:30).

† "*Doulēs*" in Luke 1:48 is the same word Mary uses in Luke 1:38 to describe herself as a "handmaiden" or "servant."

But at the same time Mary deeply understands that all these blessings in her life are not her own doing. She did not become "full of grace," the mother of the Messiah, and "blessed among women" through her own effort or because of some innate spiritual talent. Mary recognizes her lowliness, and her song underscores that all she has comes from God's grace. Notice how everything Mary says about herself in these verses is in relation to God. She seeks not to exalt herself but to magnify the Lord (Luke 1:46). She views herself as just a lowly handmaiden, a servant (*doulēs*) of the Lord (1:48). But God has come as her Savior and looked kindly on her lowliness (1:48). It is God who has done great things for her (1:49).

There is a great difference between verbal humility and experiential humility. It is easy for someone to *say*, "I'm weak. I'm a sinner. I need God in my life." But it is completely different to experience at the core of one's being the truth about how weak one really is, how totally dependent one is on God. Jesus said in the Gospel, "for apart from me you can do nothing" (John 15:5). The humble person knows how true this statement is. And he knows this not just as an abstract spiritual principle, but in his own personal experience.

Mary recognizes this truth of the human condition. She understands how small she really is. She knows that on her own she is nothing, and that she is completely dependent on the Lord. Mary thus exhibits Christ's teaching that the humble will be exalted. Only when we are convinced, like Mary was, of how little we can really do on our own and how utterly dependent we are on God can the Lord begin to act in magnificent ways in us and through us.

Mary and Israel

Another noteworthy point in the Magnificat is the theme of reversal in the first and second halves of this song. Let's consider the second part of Mary's hymn of praise.

> *He has shown strength with his arm,*
> *he has scattered the proud in the imagination of their hearts,*
> *he has put down the mighty from their thrones,*
> *and exalted those of low degree;*
> *he has filled the hungry with good things,*
> *and the rich he has sent empty away.*
> *He has helped his servant Israel,*
> *in remembrance of his mercy*
> *as he spoke to our fathers,*
> *to Abraham and to his posterity for ever.* (Luke 1:51–55)

In the first part of the Magnificat, we see how Mary focuses on the blessings God has bestowed on her personally—how the Lord has looked upon her lowliness and has done great things for her (1:46–50). In the second half Mary praises God for what he is doing for all of Israel—showing his mercy on his people, exalting all the lowly and rescuing them from their afflictions (1:51–55). This movement from lowliness to exaltation—both in Mary as an individual (first half) and in the people as a whole (second half)—is a crucial key to understanding the Magnificat. Mary does not view the blessings she has received as something for herself. She sees God's work in her life as a pattern anticipating what God wants to do for all his people. Just as God looked upon Mary's lowliness (*tapeinōsin*) (1:48) and did great things for her, so he will look upon all those of "low degree" (*tapeinous*) (1:52) and exalt them.

In the process, there will be a dramatic shake-up in the land of Israel. The hungry will be filled and the lowly raised up, while the proud will be scattered, the mighty cast down, and the rich sent away empty. Mary's song thus prophetically foreshadows her son's public ministry, which will reflect these dramatic reversals. Jesus will raise up the lowly by feeding the hungry, healing the sick, forgiving sinners, and extending fellowship to those ostracized in society; many of the political and religious leaders of the day will oppose Christ and be left out of his kingdom. Mary prophesies that God has looked mercifully on Israel's afflictions and will gather all the suffering and oppressed into the kingdom of his Son while the proud, the mighty, and the rich who oppose God's people will be cast down.

The relationship between the two halves of Mary's song is clear. The way God is working in Mary's life anticipates the saving deeds he will do for all of Israel. Just as God looked upon Mary's lowliness and exalted her, so the Lord will look mercifully upon all the downtrodden in Israel and raise them up to become heirs of the kingdom. In the Magnificat, Mary proclaims not only the good things God is doing in her own life, but Good News for all God's people.

STEP 4

Keep and Ponder

The Mother at the Manger (Luke 2:1–20)

The Mary of the Bible is not fully portrayed by the Mary of your Nativity set.

Not that the common depiction of Mary kneeling down with her head bowed over the manger and her hands folded is a false one—these portrayals beautifully highlight Mary's loving devotion to the Child she just delivered. But that's not the whole picture. A lot more happened to Mary on that first Christmas night, and Luke's account of Christ's birth gives us a deeper glimpse into Mary's soul. The narrative suggests that Mary went through many trials on her way to deliver Israel's Messiah, but she also leaves us a powerful example of how to face the crosses that come up in life: she "kept all these things, pondering them in her heart" (Luke 2:19).

Let's step back and put ourselves in Mary's situation as we walk with her through Luke's account of the Nativity story.

The Census

Mary's troubles begin with the census of Caesar. Notice how Luke's Gospel draws more attention to the census than to the actual details of Jesus's birth.

> In those days a decree went out from Caesar Augustus that all the world should be *enrolled*. This was the first *enrollment*, when Quirinius was governor of Syria. And all went to be *enrolled*, each to his own city. And Joseph also went up from Galilee, from the city of Nazareth, to Judea, to the city of David, which is called Bethlehem, because he was of the house and lineage of David, to be *enrolled* with Mary his betrothed, who was with child. (Luke 2:1–5)

Luke repeats the word *enrolled* four times in this passage. Remarkably, the description of the census is longer (Luke 2:1–5) than the narration of Christ's birth, which tells us only that Mary delivered her firstborn son, wrapped him in swaddling clothes, and laid him in a manger (Luke 2:7). Why does Luke put so much emphasis on the enrollment? And how might this Roman enrollment have affected Mary?

The enrollment was a census carried out from time to time in the Roman Empire, and it involved listing people and property for the purposes of tax assessment and military conscription. Since Jews would not be drafted into the Roman army, the focus of this decree is the Roman tribute—a disturbing symbol of Roman dominance.* The Romans used heavy taxes as a

---

*See Richard Horsley, *The Liberation of Christmas: The Infancy Narratives in Social Context* (New York: Crossroad, 1989), 34–35.

way of demeaning the people they conquered and as a revenue stream to support the imperial domination. As one Roman general explained to the Gauls after suppressing their revolt in 70 AD: "We, though so often provoked, have used the right of conquest to burden you only with the cost of maintaining peace. For the tranquility of nations cannot be preserved without armies; armies cannot exist without pay; pay cannot be furnished without tribute."*

Moreover, tribute was a sign of loyalty to Rome, and Jews in Palestine in the time of Mary and Joseph would incur the Romans' wrath if tribute was delayed. Luke's mention of the census, therefore, would be a painful reminder of Roman rule over the Jewish people.

This particular decree requires Joseph to be registered in his ancestral town, which is Bethlehem of Judea, a small city about seven miles south of Jerusalem. Assuming a Jew bypassed the hostile territory of the Samaritans, the ninety-mile journey from Nazareth to Bethlehem would have taken about four days—not a leisurely trip for most, certainly not for an expectant mother.

At the same time, Luke is also showing how there is a higher power who is really in control of human affairs. Though Caesar's decree was intended to serve the interests of the Roman Empire, God uses it so that the Messiah will be born in the proper city, Bethlehem.

---

*Tacitus, *Histories* 4.74 in *The Complete Works of Tacitus,* translated by Alfred John Church and William Jackson Brodribb (New York: Random House, 1942).

O Little Town?

Bethlehem was a small city linked with big expectations. Luke's Gospel introduces it as the "city of David" for good reason. Although Jerusalem normally holds this title in the Old Testament (2 Sam. 5:7, 9; 6:10, 12, 16; 2 Kings 9:28; 12:22), Bethlehem was at the foundation of the Davidic dynasty: it was David's city of origin and the place where David was anointed king (1 Sam. 16; 17:12, 58). Moreover, Bethlehem was associated with royal hopes for the future. The prophet Micah foretold that a future royal descendant of David would reunite the people of Israel and rule over all nations, and that this new king, like David himself, would come from the city of Bethlehem:

> But you, O Bethlehem Ephrathah,
> who are little to be among the clans of Judah,
> from you shall come forth for me one who is to be ruler in
> Israel,
> whose origin is from of old, from ancient days. (Mic. 5:2)

Here we can see that although Luke's Gospel highlights how Mary's delivery of the Christ child takes place in the context of Caesar's census and the Roman exploitation of the Jewish people, the Gospel also shows us that whatever trials Mary and Joseph might have faced in their Roman-imposed move to Bethlehem, they ultimately were brought there in God's Providence. Caesar unknowingly serves the purposes of God. The Messiah-King is born in Bethlehem, and the prophecy is fulfilled.

Where Was Jesus Born?

Where in Bethlehem did Mary give birth to Jesus? Was it in a stable? A house? A cave? Various traditions have emerged over the centuries. Luke's Gospel does not offer us much information to settle this question. Only two major clues are given: the manger and the inn.

Luke reports that Mary gave birth to Jesus and "laid him in a *manger,* because there was no place for them in *the inn*" (Luke 2:7). The mention of a manger (a feeding trough) indicates that the infant Jesus was placed in some area where animals dwell. The nature of "the inn," however, is harder to unpack. Though the Greek word *katalyma* used in Luke 2:7 is commonly translated "inn," it actually has a broader meaning that denotes any kind of lodging place. The word can refer to a primitive inn (Exod. 4:24; 1 Kings 1:18), a guest room in a house (Luke 22:11), or simply a place to stay (Sir. 14:25; cf. Exod. 15:13).

One possibility is that *katalyma* refers to a travelers' inn that existed in or near Bethlehem (see Jer. 41:17). Such an inn would be very different from a modern motel. A Palestinian inn of that era was a public shelter or caravansary where large groups of travelers lodged under one roof. Guests usually slept on cots while their animals remained on a lower level of the building or in a stable next to it. In this scenario, Mary and Joseph could not find room in a travelers' inn, so they went near the animals or to the stable so that Mary could have the baby.

Another possibility is that *katalyma* refers to the living quarters in a home. Since Joseph is traveling to his family's hometown, it might be expected that he would stay not at a traveler's inn but with relatives in Bethlehem. Palestinian peasant homes often housed people and animals under the same roof. The family would dwell on a raised platform while the animals remained on a slightly lower level, where there would be a manger. In this scenario, there was no room in the overcrowded living quarters of the home—the *katalyma*—so Mary delivered the child in the more discreet location where the animals were kept, and she laid the baby in the manger there.

A third possibility is based on an ancient tradition that Jesus was born in a cave on the outskirts of Bethlehem. As early as the second century there is evidence of Christians holding to this view.[*] So strong was this tradition in the fourth century that Constantine erected a basilica over a series of Bethlehem caves to commemorate the site where it was believed Jesus was born. This is possible since caves were commonly used to stable animals and in some cases served as dwellings for people.

Whatever the case may be, Mary certainly gave birth to Israel's Messiah in a setting unfit for a king. As John Paul II commented, "Mary experiences childbirth in a condition of extreme poverty; she could not give the Son of God even what mothers usually offer a newborn baby; instead, she has to lay him 'in a manger,' an improvised cradle which contrasts with the dignity of the 'Son of the Most High.'"[†]

Furthermore, although one might expect the birth of Israel's long-awaited king to stir great excitement and praise among the people, the newborn Christ escapes the notice of practically all the Jews in Judea. None of the Jewish religious leaders of the day come to welcome their Messiah. Not the priests. Not the

---

[*] *Protoevangelium of James* 18; Justin Martyr, *Dialogue with Trypho* 78:4; Origen, *Against Celsus* 1:51.

[†] John Paul II, General audience, November 20, 1996, in *Theotokos,* 146.

Pharisees. Not the Sadducees. Nor do any of the wealthy or governing authorities in Judea pay a visit. Only some unnamed lowly shepherds from the bottom rung of Jewish society come to witness the arrival of their Lord and King.

A Matter of the Heart

Mary had a lot to endure between traveling to Bethlehem when she was well along in her pregnancy and then giving birth among animals and laying her child in a manger. On top of all this, the birth of Israel's Messiah escapes the notice of all the leaders in Israel. Certainly, this is not the way the King should be treated!

The Bible does not give us much insight into what was stirring inside Mary during these humbling events. But it does reveal one detail. In the face of the humiliation, poverty, and rejection of her son, Mary is never shown to complain. She never says, "Hey, I'm the mother of the Messiah. All you in Bethlehem should treat our family better!" Instead Mary brings these trials into her interior life. She prayerfully "kept all these things, pondering them in her heart" (Luke 2:18).

Mary's response to these trials and humiliations can serve as a model for how we should handle the little crosses we face each day. How do you respond when *your* life is disrupted—when other people or events shake up your life and your plans suddenly have to change? How do you feel when *you* are not treated well—when you are not recognized or appreciated or given the attention you think you deserve?

Many of us become anxious when difficulties come our way. We may press the panic button and nervously fret about what will happen next. Or we may pour all our energy into fixing our life problems through our own plotting and scheming. Or we may just sulk when things are not going our way and complain when we think we're not being treated well.

Mary's example reminds us that no matter what may happen in our lives, we should always ask God what he might be trying to teach us through these crosses that come our way. Perhaps we have an opportunity to grow in patience or humility. Or maybe God wants us to grow in greater trust or surrender of our own willfulness. There will be suffering and heartache in this fallen world, but God can bring good from those difficult situations and use them to help us grow in certain ways that are for our spiritual development. So the next time something frustrating or painful happens in our lives, instead of immediately pressing the panic button, adopting the "I've got to fix this right now" attitude, or complaining, we should pray and ask God what he is trying to teach us through these crosses. We, like Mary, should *keep all these things, pondering them in our hearts.*

To Keep and Ponder in the Heart

But what does this expression mean? In the Bible the heart is more than a vital organ. It symbolizes the center of one's thoughts, desires, and attentions. All actions flow from the heart. Mary is described as keeping and pondering all these things—these mysterious events surrounding her son's birth—in her heart.

The expression "keep all these things, pondering them in her heart" points to much more than simply remembering or recalling. To ponder (*symballein*) can be literally translated as "to throw side by side." It depicts someone meditating, comparing ideas, putting his or her thoughts together into a comprehensive whole.

In the Old Testament the Greek verb meaning "to keep," *synterein,* describes someone reflecting on the meaning of profound events, especially matters of divine revelation. When the patriarch Joseph told his father and brothers of his mysterious dreams about the sun, moon, and eleven stars bowing down before him, his father Jacob "kept the saying in mind" (Gen. 37:9–11). Similarly, when the prophet Daniel interpreted King Nebuchadnezzar's dream for him, the king "kept" Daniel's explanation in his heart. Daniel himself received a vision at night and "kept" the meaning of the vision that was revealed to him in a dream (Dan. 7:28). In each of these cases the expression describes someone wanting to interpret the meaning of the vision or dream correctly.

In the Wisdom tradition of the Old Testament, the expression takes on even deeper significance. It describes someone seeking not only to interpret the message correctly but also to observe it—to live it out. We see this, for example, in Psalm 119:11: "I have laid up your word in my heart that I might not sin against you." Note how the Psalmist seeks not simply intellectual comprehension of God's word, but understanding in his heart so that he will live according to the law. Similarly in Proverbs 3:1 a father says to his son, "Let your heart keep my commandments." Again, the emphasis is on the son not only comprehending the commands of the father, but understanding them so that he may live according to his father's wise counsels. The book of Sirach makes a similar point when it describes how the wise man keeps with concern the parables and prophecies of God handed down to him (Sir. 39:1–3).

Luke's statement at the end of the Nativity story that Mary "kept all these things, pondering them in her heart," therefore, describes her as a woman who seeks to understand the deeper meaning of all the events surrounding her son's birth. Mary wants to understand what God is trying to reveal through these trials. She does not have all the answers. Why was her son born under the oppressive circumstances of the Roman census? Why was there no room for him in the inn when the time came for him to be born? Why did he enter this world in such humility and poverty? All this would cause anguish for any mother. Mary seeks to understand God's design so that she can live according to what God is trying to teach her through these trials.

Over time Mary will see even more clearly what Luke's Gospel highlights: that the way Jesus was born into the world foreshadows how he will die. Just as Jesus was born into the world in the context of humility, poverty, and suffering under Roman rule, so he will die in humiliation and poverty at the hands of the Roman authorities. Luke's Gospel, in fact, uses two key words to underscore the connection between Christ's birth in Bethlehem and his death on Calvary, and how the circumstances of one foreshadow the circumstances of the other: at his birth, Jesus is "wrapped" in swaddling clothes and "laid" in a manger (Luke 2:7); and at his death, his body is taken down from the cross to be *wrapped* in a linen shroud and *laid* in the tomb (Luke 23:53).

And Luke seems to associate Mary in particular with the theme of Christ's rejection in this verse when he says "there was no room for them in the inn." The "them" is typically understood as referring to Mary and Joseph not being able to find a good place for the child to be born. But all the focus is on Mary and the child Jesus in this verse:

> And she gave birth to her first-born son and wrapped him in swaddling clothes, and laid him in a manger, because there was no place for them in the inn. (Luke 2:7)

New Testament scholar Beverly Gaventa points out how Mary is the subject of all the verbs and the child is the recipient of all the actions in this verse. Mary gave birth to her firstborn son. Mary wrapped the child in swaddling clothes. And Mary laid the child in a manger. Gaventa explains, "Three active verbs describe the events, each of which has Mary as its subject and the babe as its object. Here Mary acts alone. . . . Even Joseph remains hidden from the narrator's vision."*

So when Luke at the end of this verse says there was no room "for them," this would most naturally point particularly to Mary and the child. If this is the case, perhaps Luke is subtly showing how Mary, already at the Nativity, shares in the suffering of her son—a theme that becomes explicit with Simeon's words at the Presentation about the sword piercing her soul (Luke 2:35). That is how John Paul II interpreted this scene:

> The Gospel notes that "there was no place for them in the inn" (Lk 2:7). This statement, recalling the text in John's Prologue: "His own people received him not" (Jn 1:11), foretells as it were the many refusals Jesus will meet with

---

*See Gaventa, *Mary: Glimpses of the Mother of Jesus*, 59–60.

during his earthly life. The phrase "for them" joins the Son and the Mother in this rejection and shows how Mary is already associated with her son's destiny of suffering and shares in his redeeming mission.[*]

Right at the beginning of her maternal mission Mary gets a taste of the affliction and rejection her son will endure. The message of the Nativity foreshadows the message of the cross. It is this message that Mary keeps and ponders and will come to understand more fully over time.

Unlike Mary, however, many of us overlook the deeper meaning of the events unfolding in our lives. This is often the case when it comes to the trials and sufferings we face. We tend to run away from the crosses that come our way. We focus more on solving all our problems, worrying about them, or complaining about them than on really praying through them to understand how the Lord's hand might be forming and guiding us through a difficult experience. Moreover, Mary reminds us that God is always trying to teach us something, even through the difficulties and sufferings we face in life. Her example teaches us that we should keep all these things and ponder them in our heart.

More than Wonder

It is also worth noting how Mary's response stands in contrast to that of the people who hear the shepherds' report about the angel's revelation. They wonder, but they do not take time to

---

[*] John Paul II, General audience, November 20, 1996, in *Theotokos*, 146.

ponder the significance of what has happened. Luke's Gospel emphasizes the difference between their superficial reaction and Mary's response: "All who heard wondered at what the shepherds told them. *But* Mary kept all these things, pondering them in her heart" (Luke 2:18).

Wonder is a typical, natural reaction to supernatural events in the Bible. Although the connotation is not negative, wonder in Luke's Gospel does not denote faith and does not always lead toward full understanding of the events at hand. During Jesus's public ministry, for example, the people in Jesus's hometown of Nazareth initially *wondered* at his preaching, but later in the same scene they want to kill him (Luke 4:22, 28–29). Mary's response at the Nativity goes far beyond simple amazement. She, unlike the hearers of the shepherds' report about the baby in the manger, stands out as a woman who does not simply react to what is happening around her and then move on to the next thing. Mary reflects interiorly on the meaning of the events in her life to discern where the Lord is leading her. She is the one who "kept all these things, pondering them in her heart"—an expression that, as Francis Moloney explains, is used in the Bible to describe someone who has received a revelation that is beyond his understanding and waits for God to show him or her the meaning in due time:

There is a mystery about the revelation whose significance he or she cannot fully grasp. In such a situation one can simply marvel, and then go one's way (see, for example, Lk 2:18) or one can "treasure in the heart." The mystery can be taken into the deepest recesses of one's being, guarded and pondered over in one's heart. The faithful ones simply await God's time and plan for the full revelation of the mysteries entrusted to them.*

This is the case with Mary. She patiently awaits further understanding.

But she won't have to wait long. Forty days after Jesus's birth, Mary receives a disturbing revelation from the prophet Simeon that sheds more light on her son's suffering and rejection—and serves as the next significant step in her journey with the Lord.

---

*Moloney, *Mary: Woman and Mother*, 24.

Sharing in the Sword

———— ✳ ————

Mary's Participation in Her Son's Sufferings
(Luke 2:22–40)

The next step in Mary's faith journey takes her to the Jerusalem Temple—the sacred place where Jews offered their sacrifices to God. Little did she know that during her visit there she would hear a prophecy of her participation in a sacrifice of untold magnitude. Indeed, she would be called upon to share in the greatest sacrifice a mother could experience: the offering of her son.

Mary arrives at the Temple with a much lesser sacrifice on her mind: just a small amount of money and two birds.

The Jewish law required Mary to present her firstborn son to God at the Temple and offer five shekels to support the priests. She was also coming to offer a sacrifice for herself. As a woman who had just given birth, she would be considered ritually impure for forty days. When the time for her purification was completed, the law called for her to offer a lamb and a young pigeon to the priests at the Temple. If a woman could not afford a lamb, she could instead present a pair of young pigeons or turtledoves. The fact that Mary offered the pair of turtledoves (Luke 2:24) tells us she was among the poor. She could not afford the lamb.

Five shekels and two birds were the only sacrifices she was planning to offer as she entered the Temple that day. But everything changed when a man named Simeon appeared and announced to Mary the difficult journey that lay ahead for her child—and for her.

Simeon's Prophecy

Simeon stands out as a model Jew. He is "righteous and devout" and longing for God's plan of salvation to be fulfilled (Luke 2:25). The Holy Spirit was upon him, and therefore he prophesied. Most remarkable is that he has been given an extraordinary message from God: the Holy Spirit revealed to Simeon that he would not die until he saw the Messiah. His whole life, therefore, is bound up with the great expectation that one day he will meet Israel's Savior-King.

Imagine the scene from Mary's perspective. As she and Joseph arrive at the Jerusalem Temple, this complete stranger approaches them and suddenly takes the child into his arms. Then, holding the Christ child up in the air, Simeon begins blessing God, saying,

> *Lord, now let your servant depart in peace,*
> *according to your word;*
> *for mine eyes have seen your salvation*
> *which you have prepared in the presence of all peoples,*

a light for revelation to the Gentiles,
and for glory to your people Israel. (Luke 2:29–32)

What an astonishing moment this must have been for Mary! First of all, she has no idea who this man is and why he is reaching for her baby. But as Simeon holds the child up and begins to speak, he describes the future greatness of this child with words that would have seemed encouraging to Mary and rounded out the picture for her about her royal son's mission. Simeon describes the child as God's "salvation" and as "a light of revelation to the Gentiles"—images that recall prophecies from the book of Isaiah. The prophet Isaiah foretold that "all the ends of the earth shall see the salvation of our God" (Isa. 52:10; cf. Isa. 40:5). Simeon proclaims he has seen in the Christ child that very salvation that Isaiah prophesied. Isaiah also prophesied about how God would send a redeemer figure, the servant of the Lord, to be "a light to the nations" (Isa. 42:6; 49:6). Simeon's words, therefore, announce that the child in his arms is the one who will carry out the Lord's universal mission to the nations. He will be "a light for revelation to the Gentiles," the one fulfilling the prophecies of Isaiah.

The Second Annunciation

All this would have left Mary in awe. Indeed, Luke tells us she and Joseph "marveled at what was said about [their child]" (Luke 2:33). Simeon's next prophecy, however, would give Mary reason to pause. He singles out Mary and addresses her with ominous words about the child's future rejection and the suffering she will face:

> *Behold, this child is set for the fall and rising of*
>   *many in Israel,*
> *and for a sign that is spoken against*
> *(and a sword will pierce through your own soul also),*
> *that thoughts out of many hearts may be revealed.*
> (Luke 2:34–35)

John Paul II described Simeon's prophecy as "a second annunciation to Mary."[*] At Nazareth, at the first Annunciation, Mary learned that she would become the mother of Israel's Messiah. Now through Simeon's words in the Temple—in this "second annunciation"—she gets a much clearer picture of what she signed up for nine months and forty days earlier. These words, John Paul II writes, "tell her of the actual historical situation in which the Son is to accomplish his mission, namely, in misunderstanding and sorrow. . . . [This announcement] also reveals to her that she will have to live her obedience of faith in suffering, at the side of the suffering Savior, and that her motherhood will be mysterious and sorrowful."[†]

Simeon's message to Mary contains four statements about the fate that she and her son will suffer. First Simeon says that the child is destined for "the fall and rising of many in Israel" (Luke 2:34). These words point to great turmoil surrounding Jesus's future ministry. And they echo the theme of reversal found in Mary's song (the Magnificat): Mary announced that the rich and the mighty will be cast down while the poor, the hungry, and the lowly will be exalted (Luke 1:51–55). Simeon's

---

[*] John Paul II, *Redemptoris Mater,* 16.
[†] Ibid., 16.

prophecy picks up that theme and anticipates the different responses to Christ's Proclamation of the Kingdom. Many of the sick, the poor, and other covenant outsiders will be exalted and welcomed into Christ's kingdom, while many of the religious and political leaders of Jesus's day will oppose him and be cast down because they reject the Kingdom of God he offers them.

Next, Simeon says that Jesus will be "a sign that is spoken against." This language does not suggest someone being merely criticized or mocked. The Greek word for "spoken against," *antilego,* is always used by Luke in the context of Jewish opposition to Christ (Luke 20:27, 21:15) and his disciples (Acts 4:14, 13:45, 28:22). When read in the wider context of Luke's Gospel and the Acts of the Apostles, Simeon's words foreshadow the hostile opposition Jesus and his followers will face.

But the image that best portrays the future suffering of Christ is that of the sword. The way Simeon uses this image tells Mary two things. First, she would realize that in some sense a sword will pierce her son, Jesus. In the Old Testament a sword can symbolize war, bloodshed, and death (see Gen. 27:40; Lev. 26:6; Deut. 32:25; Josh. 5:13; Isa. 1:20). Simeon's image of a sword piercing Jesus is both figurative and literal, since it points to both the violent opposition Christ's ministry will provoke as well as the horrible death he will suffer on the cross, after which a Roman soldier will pierce his side with a sword (John 19:34).

Second, Mary would also get the message that this hostile opposition to Christ will affect her: "a sword will pierce through your own soul also" (Luke 2:35). The Greek word Luke employs for sword, *rhomphaia,* is a vivid one. The sword envisioned here is not a pocketknife or small dagger. The word denotes a very large, broad, two-edged sword. The picture of

such a weapon passing through Mary's soul graphically illuminates the intense emotional suffering she will endure as a result
of her son's rejection.

That Luke is linking Mary with the suffering of her son is
made even clearer when we consider that Psalm 22 lies in the
background of both Simeon's words to Mary and Luke's narration of Christ's passion.

Psalm 22 portrays the persecution of a righteous man who
suffers greatly at the hands of his enemies. He is described in
ways that foreshadow Christ's torment on Good Friday (Luke
23:35–39). The man's hands and feet are pierced (Ps. 22:16).
His garments are divided (Ps. 22:18). And his enemies mock
him and then cast lots for his clothing (Ps. 22:7, 18). All this
happens also to the righteous Jesus, who is unjustly condemned
to death by his enemies. His hands and feet are nailed to the
cross and his enemies cast lots for his garments.

Psalm 22 also seems to be a key backdrop to Simeon's words
to Mary. The Psalmist states, "Deliver my *soul* from the *sword*"
(Psalm 22:20), and Simeon says to Mary in Luke 2:35 that "a
sword will pierce through your own *soul,* also." This connection is especially clear when comparing Simeon's words in Luke
with this Psalm in the Septuagint, the most ancient translation of the Old Testament Scriptures into Greek. Both texts use
the same two key words—*rhomphaia* (large sword) and *psychē*
(soul)—and both involve the context of hostile opposition. In
this way, Luke links Mary with Jesus's rejection and passion. As
commentator Michael Goulder explains, "[Luke's] thought is
of her son's coming rejection by his people, and he thinks what
this will mean to her too, especially in the crucifixion; he has
taken the image from Ps. 22 because that is where the Passion

prophecies come, and the sword that will pass through Mary's soul can have no other meaning than this."[*] Goulder continues, "She is to suffer the pain of the sign that is spoken against also, and Luke, thinking especially of the cross, applies to her a text from Ps. 22 (LXX 21.21), 'Save my soul from the sword (*rouphaias*).'"[†]

Mary, thus, gains a fuller understanding of just how difficult her mission will be. At her fiat she consented to become the mother of the Messiah. Now she realizes that her maternal mission will be fraught with suffering. Her fiat in Nazareth will ultimately lead her to Calvary, where she will sorrowfully look on as her son dies on the cross to fulfill his messianic mission.

Think about what this revelation would have meant for Mary. Imagine being a new mother, holding your infant in your arms and suddenly being told by a prophet that one day your child will face hostile opposition and be killed. Imagine having to carry that burden with you every day as you raise your child, knowing that at some time after your son has grown up, the fierce antagonism toward him will begin—an opposition that will only increase and reach its climax in your son's violent death.

If we were in Mary's shoes, we might have second thoughts about proceeding with our mission. If we had received such a clear picture of the trials that lay ahead, we might hesitate about moving forward. But Mary does not waver from her calling, even in the face of this ominous "second annunciation." She

---

[*] Michael Goulder, *Luke: A New Paradigm* (*Journal for the Study of the New Testament*), vol. 1, Supp. 20 (Sheffield, UK: Sheffield Academic Press, 1989), 260. See also Nolland, *Luke 1:1–9:20*, 122.

[†] Ibid., 259.

doesn't pull back and say, "This is not what I was expecting. This is too much to ask. I want out." Mary continues her walk with the Lord.

The Soul and the Sword

One last reflection: Simeon speaks of Mary's soul (*psychē*), which in the Bible refers to the vital principle of a human being and the very source of human consciousness and freedom. He tells her that something devastating will happen to her right there at the core of her being: a sword will pierce her soul.

Interestingly, Mary is the only person in Luke's Gospel whose soul is mentioned and described.* And Luke refers to Mary's soul not just once, but twice. The first mention of Mary's soul is in the Magnificat, when Mary says, "My soul [*psychē*] magnifies the Lord" (Luke 1:46). The second and only other mention of Mary's soul is here in the Presentation scene where Simeon says to her, "a sword will pierce your soul [*psychē*] also." If one were to view these two references to Mary's soul together, perhaps the following spiritual reflection could be drawn out: Mary's soul magnifies God the most by participating in the sword of Christ's sufferings. In the Magnificat we learn that Mary's soul magnifies, makes great, the Lord. In the Presentation scene, we learn more about *how* her soul magnifies the Lord, how her

---

*All the other uses of soul (*psychē*) in Luke's Gospel do not refer to a particular human person. Most of the time the term is used by Jesus in various teachings—about saving life (6:9; 9:24; 17:33; 21:19); about loving God with all your soul (10:27); and about hating one's life in the sense of making discipleship a priority over all other human concerns (14:26). Luke also uses the term to describe the man in the parable of the rich fool who stores up grain for himself (Luke 12:19–20).

soul gives God the most praise when it shares in the sacrificial love of her son—in other words, when her soul is pierced by the sword.

This connection reminds us that we are all called to be like Mary and follow Jesus to the cross. If we desire to magnify God in our souls, we, too, must be willing to draw near to Christ's cross and be pierced by the sword. Jesus is looking for souls who are willing to follow him in his passion. In the Gospels, large crowds flock to Jesus to watch his spectacular miracles, to receive healing, or to be fed from his multiplication of loaves. But few seek out Jesus in his passion and draw near to him on Calvary. Even most of his closest friends, the apostles, abandon him on Good Friday. Mary is one of the few who draw near to Jesus in his darkest hour when the "sword" falls upon him.

"Be the One"

Mother Teresa often reflected on the mystery of Christ's solitude and abandonment on Good Friday. She would look at a holy card depicting the beaten Jesus scourged and crowned with thorns. Printed on the holy card were the following words from Psalm 68:21, which traditionally have been seen as pointing to Christ's experience in his passion: "I looked for one that would comfort me and I found none." Mother Teresa loved to gaze at this image and ponder Christ seeking unsuccessfully for someone to comfort him. She desired to be the one who would be with him, so she wrote on the card, "Be the one." She gave copies of the card to her followers and exhorted them to join her in this aspiration.

Tell Jesus, "I will be the one." I will comfort, encourage and
love him. . . . Be with Jesus. He prayed and prayed, and then
he went to look for consolation, but there was none. . . . I
always write that sentence, "I looked for one to comfort Me,
but I found no one." Then I write, "Be the one." So now you
be that one. Try to be the one to share with him, to comfort
him, to console him. So let us ask Our Lady to help us understand.[*]

But if we dare to "be the one"—if we dare to draw near to
Jesus on the cross as Mother Teresa aspired to do and as Mary
did—that means we, too, will experience the sword of Christ's
suffering. In a letter to one of her sisters, Mother Teresa said,
"Suffering, pain—failure—is but a kiss of Jesus, a sign that you
have come so close to Jesus on the Cross that He can kiss you."
She explained in another letter, "I think this is the most beautiful definition of suffering.—So let us be happy when Jesus
stoops down to kiss us.—I hope we are close enough that He
can do that."[†] Similarly, she told her sisters that their vocation
to be a spouse of Jesus Christ would entail sharing in his love
on the cross: "Your parents must have kissed you as a real sign
of love. If I am the spouse of Jesus crucified, He has to kiss me.
Naturally, the nails will hurt me. If I come close to the crown
of thorns it will hurt me."[‡]

Through Simeon's prophecy, Mary sees more clearly where
the future will lead her. The sword is on her horizon. As Christ's

---

[*] Mother Teresa, *Come Be My Light*, 260–61.

[†] Ibid., 282, 281.

[‡] Ibid., 282.

mother she will share, more than anyone else, in this "kiss" of her son's suffering. In the face of this startling revelation at her "second annunciation," Mary's response is still the same; she still says yes as the servant of the Lord, regardless of the cost. She, in fact, will "be the one" who will draw near to her son's cross and experience the sword more than anyone else.

Walking in Darkness

————❖————

She Who Did Not Understand (Luke 2:41–52)

I t is remarkable that the only event from Christ's childhood recorded in the New Testament seems to be an embarrassing one for Mary and Joseph.

> Now his parents went to Jerusalem every year at the feast of the Passover. And when he was twelve years old, they went up according to custom; and when the feast was ended, as they were returning, the boy Jesus stayed behind in Jerusalem. His parents did not know it, but supposing him to be in the company they went a day's journey, and they sought him among their kinsfolk and acquaintances; and when they did not find him, they returned to Jerusalem, seeking him. (Luke 2:41–45)

At first glance this account seems scandalous! How could Mary and Joseph forget their twelve-year-old boy, leaving him behind in the big city of Jerusalem? What kind of parents would do such a thing?

Even more astonishing is that out of the many details the Bible could have revealed to us about Jesus's childhood, this is the only scene from Jesus's "hidden years" narrated by any of the Gospels. From Jesus's presentation in the Temple as a forty-day-old infant to his appearance at the Jordan River where he is baptized as a thirty-year-old man, Luke's Gospel tells us nothing about Jesus's life—except this one event when he was lost and then found in the Temple.

Why was this single event so important for Luke? And what might it tell us about Jesus and his mother?

Negligent Parents?

The Old Testament Law required Jewish men to make a pilgrimage to the Temple in Jerusalem for three of Israel's main feasts: Passover, Pentecost, and Tabernacles (see Deut. 16:16). Because of the scattering of the Jewish people in the first century, Jews living farther away from Jerusalem probably made the trip only once a year. Luke notes that it was customary for Jesus's parents to make their annual pilgrimage for the feast of Passover: "His parents went to Jerusalem every year at the feast of the Passover" (Luke 2:41). It's noteworthy that Mary is mentioned as making the pilgrimage each year. Men were required to go, but women were not. For Mary to go year after year is a sign of her devotion to the Lord.[*]

---

[*] Darrell Bock, *Luke 1.1–9:50,* vol. 1, *Baker Exegetical Commentary on the New Testament,* ed. Moisés Silva (Grand Rapids, Mich.: Baker Books, 1994), 264.

The eighty-mile journey from Nazareth to Jerusalem would have taken three to four days, and people usually traveled there for the feasts in large caravans. Relatives, friends, and neighbors could share resources and assist one another. Traveling in a larger group offered protection from highway robbers. Within the large crowd of travelers, people moved at different paces, some slower than others, but the whole group would meet at the end of the day to rest together for the night.

Since extended family often shared responsibility for watching over the children, it would not be surprising for parents to assume that fellow kinsmen were taking care of their child. That seems to be the case with Mary and Joseph: "Supposing him to be in the company [the caravan] they went a day's journey, and they sought him among their kinsfolk and acquaintances" (Luke 2:44). Only at the end of the day, when everyone was gathered together for the night, did Mary and Joseph realize their son was missing, and they rushed back to Jerusalem in search of him.

The Search

Their search was a long one. Finally on the third day they discover Jesus seated among the teachers in the Temple, listening to them and asking them questions. As a twelve-year-old boy, Jesus would not yet have been considered, according to the law, fully responsible before the Lord. That would happen at age thirteen. Nevertheless, the young Jesus impresses the elders of the Temple, who are "*amazed* at his understanding and his answers." The word Luke employs for *amazed, existanto,* describes the marvel associated with someone encountering God's presence. Luke, therefore, depicts the elders in the Temple as being in awe over such a young boy being so gifted by God. They perceive a unique endowment of wisdom from God in this twelve-year-old.

Mary and Joseph also respond to this scene with awe—but their amazement is of a different nature. Luke, in fact, uses a different word, *explagēan*, which he elsewhere uses to describe someone being overwhelmed by the power of God made manifest in teaching (Luke 4:32); or in expelling demons (Luke 9:43); or an enemy of the faith being struck blind (Acts 13:12). Mary and Joseph are overwhelmed by a feeling of heightened anxiety over the child's safety after the three-day separation, and that feeling stands in stark contrast to what they witness in the Temple precincts: their son being completely consumed by other matters with the teachers of the day, seemingly unaware of the pain this separation from his parents has caused them.

Shocked, Mary addresses Jesus: "Son, why have you treated us so? Behold, your father and I have been looking for you anxiously" (Luke 2:48). That last word, *anxiously*, in Greek, *odynomenoi*, helps us catch a glimpse of the trauma Mary and Joseph underwent during those three days of searching. The Greek word describes a deep spiritual or mental anguish. Interestingly, it is used sometimes in the Jewish tradition to depict the terror parents experience when losing a child.

Tobias, for example, tells his new father-in-law that he must leave for home at once, for his father is counting the days until his return. Tobias says, "and if I delay long he will be greatly distressed" (Tob. 9:4). Indeed, the book of Tobit goes on to narrate how Tobias's delay does cause his father great anguish and how his mother fears she will never see her son again. Similarly, in a first-century Jewish text called 4 Maccabees, a mother who witnesses the martyrdom of her seven sons rejoices that her husband did not live to experience her anguish (*odynoun*) over seeing all of her sons killed.* Mary and Joseph's anguish could be viewed along similar lines. Like the parents of Tobias and the mother of the martyrs in Maccabees, Mary and Joseph also experience great anguish when they lose their son for three days in Jerusalem.

"My Father's House"

Imagine how Mary was feeling in this scene. For three days she searches anxiously throughout Jerusalem for her lost son, only to find him engrossed with the teachers in the Temple and seemingly unaware of the grief his disappearance has caused his parents. When she asks Jesus the understandable question, "Why have you treated us so?" rather than answering her question, the twelve-year-old boy responds with cryptic questions of his own: "How is it that you sought me? Did you not know that I must be in my Father's house?" (Luke 2:49).

Luke tells us that Mary and Joseph "did not understand the saying which he spoke to them" (2:50). Mary may be thankful to be reunited with her son, but she is left puzzled by the mystery of this traumatic event. What just happened? Why did she lose Jesus for three days? And what is the meaning of her twelve-year-old boy speaking of an urgent need to be in "my Father's house"?

Let's explore the meaning of Jesus's mysterious response to

---

* 4 Macc. 18:9, as noted in Gaventa, *Mary: Glimpses of the Mother of Jesus*, 68.

Mary. First, notice the contrast Jesus makes between his earthly father and his Father in heaven. Mary speaks to Jesus of "your father" in reference to Joseph, while Jesus responds by speaking of "my Father," meaning the heavenly Father. Jesus certainly will honor and obey his earthly parents—a point Luke makes in 2:51. But he is God's Son first, and his number one commitment is to his heavenly Father.

Also significant are Jesus's words about needing to be in his Father's house. Since the Temple was commonly known as God's house, Jesus's words are sometimes interpreted as a reference to the Temple in Jerusalem where he was found. But there is more here than a focus on a sacred building. The expression also could be translated "my Father's affairs" or "my Father's business." Since the idea of a "household" in the ancient Greco-Roman world denoted not just a place but a family authority, Jesus's words refer not only to his visiting the physical house of the Lord—the Jerusalem Temple—but also to Jesus's firm commitment to pursue the work of his heavenly Father. He must be about his Father's affairs.

Hearing these words, Mary and Joseph are challenged to reflect more deeply on their twelve-year-old boy's unique intimacy with the heavenly Father. And they are being called to cooperate in their son's mission by letting him go wherever the Father might lead him—even if it causes them distress.

Mary's "Renewed Fiat"

This encounter with her son in the Temple represents another major step in Mary's journey of faith. Even though she has been given more revelation about Jesus than anyone else, Mary does not fully comprehend the significance of all that has just taken place. Luke tells us that she still had to walk by faith and seek deeper understanding. She "kept all these things in her heart" (Luke 2:51). Mary surrenders to the mystery of this event, and her commitment to keep and ponder this in her heart makes up what John Paul II calls Mary's "renewed 'fiat.'"*

John Paul II describes this scene as a significant turning point for Mary. Up to this point Mary has related to Jesus primarily as his mother, carrying the child in her womb, giving birth to him in Bethlehem, and presenting him in the Temple as a forty-day-old infant. Along the way her heart has experienced distress from various events surrounding her child's infancy: Caesar's exploitative census, no room for the child at the inn, the poor and humble conditions of her son's birth, Simeon's prophecy about the future rejection and killing of her son. Incidents of this kind would cause any mother grief.

But now, twelve years later, Mary begins to relate to her son in a new way as she is confronted with Jesus's mission to do the will of the Father. And it is no longer some external circumstance but her son himself who causes her anguish and uncertainty. As Jesus is pursuing his Father's business, his actions cause her pain, and she does not understand. The mother of Jesus is now being invited to cooperate in her son's mission to do the work of the Father.

John Paul II explains that Mary pondered these events, "offering her cooperation in the spirit of a renewed 'fiat.' In this way the first link was forged in a chain of events that would gradually lead Mary beyond the natural role deriving from her

---

*John Paul II, General audience of January 15, 1997, in *Theotokos*, 167.

motherhood, to put herself at the service of her divine son's mission."[*]

Preview of the Passion

Eventually, Mary would have discerned what Luke later highlights in his Gospel—that this one scene from Christ's childhood prefigures another time when Mary will be separated from her son: at the cross.

Indeed, this scene from Jesus's childhood connects the dots between Jesus's infancy and his public ministry. Mary's anguish over losing Jesus for three days while he pursues the business of his Father's house is an initial installment of what Simeon prophesied to Mary about a sword piercing her soul. On the other hand, the pain Mary endures in this scene anticipates the more bitter suffering she will face when she is separated from her son on Good Friday. Indeed, Luke's Gospel shows how this scene pre-enacts Christ's passion, death, and resurrection.

Consider all that happens in this passage. Jesus goes with his parents on a *pilgrimage* from *Galilee to Jerusalem,* to celebrate the feast of *Passover.* Once in the holy city, Jesus goes to the *Temple,* and while there he amazes the people with his understanding. But he ends up being *separated from his mother* because he is *doing the will of his Father,* and this causes his mother grief, until she is reunited with him on the *third day.*

All this foreshadows the climax of Christ's public ministry when Jesus makes one last pilgrimage—during which he retraces the steps of his childhood as he journeys again from

---

[*]John Paul II, General audience, January 15, 1997, in *Theotokos,* 167–68.

Galilee to Jerusalem (Luke 9:51) for the feast of *Passover* (Luke 22:7–8). And once again he goes to the *Temple* during this festival time and displays his wisdom there, this time in the role of a teacher (Luke 21:37). And *Mary loses her son* again as he pursues the will of the Father, but this time she is separated from him by his crucifixion on Calvary. And similar to what happened in his youth, Jesus is found on *the third day*—this time when he rises from the dead. Both events in Jesus's life— his being found in the Temple and his resurrection—are linked by Luke's reference to the three days that ensued (Luke 2:46; 24:7).

But the connections between the two scenes run even deeper. Both accounts involve seeking one who is lost: Mary and Joseph seek the child Jesus who is lost in Jerusalem; on Easter morning the women followers of Jesus go to the tomb seeking to anoint their master's body but find that he is not there. Moreover, both groups are asked a sharp question: the child Jesus asks his parents, "How is it that you sought me?" (Luke 2:49), while the angel asks the women at the tomb, "Why do you seek the living among the dead?" (Luke 24:5). Finally, both scenes involve remembering. After hearing the mysterious words of the child Jesus and returning home with him, Mary "kept all these things in her heart," while the women after encountering the angel at the tomb, "remembered his [Jesus's] words" about rising on the third day.[*]

By going through these dramatic events, which foreshadow Christ's passion, Mary is brought deeper into the mystery of

---

[*] See Luke Timothy Johnson, *The Gospel of Luke: Sacra Pagina* (Collegeville: Liturgical Press, 1991), 61–62.

her son's work of redemption. Over these three days, she experiences the mystery of suffering turned to joy in a way that anticipates Christ's death and resurrection.

In the Annunciation and Visitation, Mary's role is that of the mother of the Messiah. But gradually we see that the mother is being invited to share in the cross of her son and to participate in his redemptive mission. At her son's birth in the poor and humble conditions in Bethlehem, Mary experiences some initial sufferings associated with her son's rejection. At the Presentation, she learns from Simeon how she will share in the sufferings Jesus will face: a sword will pierce her soul also. But now, when Jesus is twelve, Mary directly experiences the distress of being separated from her son for three days, and then learns from him that this was all a part of the Father's plan—he must do the will of the Father. John Paul II taught that Jesus, by remaining in Jerusalem, was preparing Mary for her unique cooperation in the mystery of redemption.

> At the Temple in Jerusalem, in this prelude to his saving mission, Jesus associates his Mother with himself; no longer is she merely the one who gave him birth, but the Woman who, through her own obedience to the Father's plan, can co-operate in the mystery of Redemption.
>
> Thus keeping in her heart an event so charged with meaning, Mary attained a new dimension of her co-operation in salvation.[*]

---

[*] John Paul II, General audience, January 15, 1997, in *Theotokos*, 167–68.

When We Lose Jesus

This scene can teach us an important lesson. Like Mary, we may experience times in our relationship with Jesus when we feel anxious, unsure of where he is, and don't understand what he is doing. Whether we are suffering trials in life, uncertainty about where he is leading us, or dryness in prayer, certain circumstances may cause us to feel that Jesus is distant and lost to us. We search for him, but he is seemingly nowhere to be found.

This scene reminds us that Jesus is always doing the will of the Father, and his work sometimes causes us—as it did Mary—pain. In moments when it feels as if Jesus is lost and we "do not understand" what is happening, we should adopt the attitude of Mary who did not panic but instead prayerfully "kept all these things in her heart" (Luke 2:51). Mary trusted that there was a purpose to her ordeal, a spiritual lesson she was being invited to learn. And she believed God would reveal to her the meaning of her pain and darkness in due time. We, too, should have confidence that, even in the moments when Jesus seems far away, he is truly doing the work of his Father in the temple of our souls.

She Still Says Yes

------ ❋ ------

Mary's Choice at Cana (John 2:1–11)

Running out of refreshments at a party or not having enough hamburgers for a summer cookout might be an embarrassing moment for a modern-day host. But running short of wine at an ancient Jewish wedding feast would be a social catastrophe that could severely damage a family's reputation for years to come.

According to customs of the time, a first-century Jewish wedding was not a private family celebration, but a public event, recognizing the union of the bride and groom as well as the joining of the two families. The celebration typically took place in the groom's home, which was opened to guests for several days and thus displayed for public scrutiny.[*]

It was the responsibility of the groom's family to ensure

------

*On first-century Jewish weddings, see Bruce Malina and Richard Rohrbaugh, *Social-Science Commentary on the Gospel of John* (Minneapolis: Fortress Press, 1998); Ritva Williams, "The Mother of Jesus at Cana: A Social-Science Interpretation of John 2:1–12," *Catholic Biblical Quarterly*, vol. 59, no. 1 (Oct. 1997): 679–92.

there was enough food and drink for all the people. To fulfill this public social role, most families needed to draw on not only their own family resources but also the resources of colleagues from their social group. How well the feast went communicated to the guests the family's social status and honor. To run out of wine at a wedding feast would have inflicted grave humiliation on the groom's family, signaling that they were unable to fulfill their role as hosts adequately and that they lacked the social connections to preserve their honor.

This social context sheds much light on the crisis facing the bride and groom at the wedding feast of Cana. But it also gives us insight into Mary's role in this scene. Mary is the first to notice the impending disaster. She alone is aware of what is about to unfold, and she brings this crisis to the one person who can solve the problem: Jesus.

The Catholic tradition has seen in this event Mary's compassion and attentiveness to others' needs. The Vatican II document *Lumen Gentium* describes Mary at Cana being "moved with pity."[*] John Paul II said Mary was "prompted by her merciful heart" to help this family by bringing her concern for them to Jesus. "Having sensed the eventual disappointment of the newly married couple and guests because of the lack of wine, the Blessed Virgin compassionately suggests to Jesus that he intervene with his messianic power."[†]

Catholics have often seen in this passage a pattern for Marian intercession. Just as Mary at Cana noticed the family's needs

---

[*] *Lumen Gentium* (November 21, 1964), 58.
[†] John Paul II, General audience, March 5, 1997, in *Theotokos*, 177.

before anyone else did, so Mary in heaven continues to notice our needs before we do. And just as Mary at Cana brought those needs to Christ, so even now she continues to bring our needs to her son through her intercession for us. John Paul II once said this scene at Cana exemplifies *"Mary's solicitude for human beings,* her coming to them in the wide variety of their wants and needs." He continues:

> At Cana in Galilee there is shown only one concrete aspect of human need, apparently a small one of little importance ("They have no wine"). But it has a symbolic value: this coming to the aid of human needs means, at the same time, bringing those needs within the radius of Christ's messianic mission and salvific power. . . . Mary places herself between her son and mankind in the reality of their wants, needs and sufferings.[*]

No Wine, but Much Faith

Mary's statement to Jesus—"they have no wine" (John 2:3)—also reveals her great faith. Jesus is simply a guest at the wedding. He is not responsible for the festivities, nor does he have any wine at his disposal. From a human perspective, therefore, Jesus is not the person to whom one would turn for help. A more natural choice would be the steward in charge of the feast, the servants, or the bride and groom's family.

Nevertheless, Mary's instinct is to turn to Jesus in this

---

[*] John Paul II, *Redemptoris Mater,* 21.

predicament. She says, "They have no wine" (John 2:3). She believes Jesus can do something about this and hopes he will perform some kind of extraordinary work to avert the catastrophe.

What makes Mary's faith in Jesus most striking is the fact that up to this point in the Gospel story he has yet to perform any public miracles. Yet she still has faith in his supernatural power and believes he can help. In this way Mary anticipates the great faith Jesus spoke about to the apostle Thomas: "Blessed are those who have not seen and yet believe" (John 20:29). As one commentator has written, "Our Lord's words to Thomas apply exactly to Mary's attitude at the wedding feast of Cana; she had never seen a miracle, but she believed."* John Paul II made a similar point: Mary here precedes the faith of the disciples who will come to believe in Jesus only *after* they have witnessed the miracle of water being changed into wine (John 2:11). Mary, on the other hand, believed in Jesus's supernatural power *before* she ever saw it manifest (John 2:3–5).†

Pushing Mary Away?

Next, we come to one of the most perplexing utterances directed at Mary in the Bible. After Mary tells Jesus, "They have no wine," Jesus responds by saying, "O woman, what have you to do with me? My hour has not yet come" (John 2:4).

At first glance these words seem harsh—as if Jesus is pushing

---

*Jean Galot, *Mary in the Gospel,* trans. Sister Maria Constance (Westminster, Md.: Newman Press, 1965), 116.

†John Paul II, General audience, February 26, 1997, in *Theotokos,* 174.

away his mother. Imagine, in our twenty-first-century world, a mother calling her son to the table for supper, and the son responding by saying, "*Woman* . . . What have you to do with me? My hour has not yet come!" From our modern perspective, these words sound more like what we'd expect to hear from a rebellious teenager than the words of the holy Son of God!

But if we consider what Jesus says in light of ancient Jewish culture and in the wider context of the wedding feast at Cana, four facts emerge that make it abundantly clear that these words reflect no hostile opposition between Jesus and Mary, but rather something positive, indeed something beautiful, about their relationship.

First, in John's Gospel Jesus uses the title "woman" to politely address women with whom he has a positive relationship. This is seen, for example, when Jesus tenderly appears to Mary Magdalene on Easter Sunday (John 20:15), when Jesus forgives the sins of the woman who committed adultery (John 8:10), and when Jesus draws the Samaritan woman to faith in the Messiah (John 4:21). Given the positive way this address appears in John's Gospel, Jesus's calling Mary "woman" does not indicate a rebuke or lack of affection.

Second, in biblical times a man might address a female as "woman," but nowhere else in the ancient Greco-Roman world or in ancient Israel do we know of an example of a son addressing his mother with this title. Jesus addressing his own mother as "woman" seems to be unique in all of antiquity. This suggests that Jesus has some particular purpose in mind when he calls his *mother* "woman"—a purpose that goes beyond the normal, congenial way he addresses other women. When applied to Mary, this title "woman" likely has some important, symbolic meaning (which we will see below).[*]

Third, consider how Mary interprets Jesus's words: Does she walk away from the scene feeling sad, hurt, or rejected in any way? No, just the opposite. She hears Jesus's words and immediately says to the servants, "Do whatever he tells you" (John 2:5). Mary interprets Christ's response so positively that she confidently believes Jesus is going to fulfill her request, and she tells the servants to be ready to do whatever her son commands.

Finally, Jesus's subsequent actions indicate that he looks with favor on Mary's petition. Not only does he fulfill her request; he supplies much more wine than Mary or anyone at the feast ever would have imagined. Each of the six stone jars used for ritual purification (John 2:6) would have held 15 to 24 gallons of water. Thus, when Jesus asks that those jars be filled and then changes all that water into wine, he ends up providing some 120 gallons of wine for the wedding party. If that tremendous overabundance is meant to be a *rejection* of Mary's request, it is hard to imagine what *fulfillment* would look like! Far from denying Mary's appeal, Jesus responds in a way that exceeds all expectations.

A New Creation Week

Therefore, whatever Jesus's words "Woman, what have you to do with me" may mean, they do not imply a negative interaction between Jesus and Mary. Instead, the way Jesus addresses

---

[*] Cf. Raymond Brown, *The Gospel of John, I–XII,* Anchor Bible Series, vol. 29 (New York: Anchor Bible/Random House, 1966), 99.

his mother reveals her to be the most important woman in salvation history. Let us now consider the title "woman" in light of the opening of John's Gospel:

> *In the beginning was the Word, and the Word was with God, and the Word was God. He was in the beginning with God; all things were made through him, and without him was not anything made that was made. In him was life, and the life was the light of men. The light shines in the darkness, and the darkness has not overcome it.* (John 1:1–5)

Much of the imagery used in these opening lines recalls the story of the Creation in the book of Genesis. John starts with the words "In the beginning," which harkens back to the very first line of the Bible: "*In the beginning* God created the heavens and the earth" (Gen. 1:1). The first chapter of the Gospel of John continues this theme of creation in the next four verses, which speak of light, life, creation, and light shining in darkness—once again, images taken right out of the Creation story in the first chapter of Genesis (John 1:2–5). By drawing on these themes from Genesis, John introduces the story of Jesus against the backdrop of the Creation, highlighting how Jesus comes to bring about a renewal of all creation.

Some scholars have noted how John's Gospel continues this creation theme by setting up a series of days, which establish a new creation week.[*] After the phrase "In the beginning," John then demarcates a second day in 1:29 with the words "The next day." He then uses the same phrase to note a third

---

[*] See, for example, Ignace de la Potterie, *Mary in the Mystery of the Covenant*, 165.

day in 1:35 ("The next day") and a fourth day in 1:43 (The next day"). Finally, after these first four days, the story of the wedding at Cana is introduced as taking place three days later: "*On the third day* there was a marriage at Cana" (2:1). The third day after the fourth day would represent the seventh day in the Gospel of John. Consequently, the wedding at Cana takes place at the climax of the new creation week, the seventh day.

The New Eve

By highlighting that the wedding feast of Cana takes place on the seventh day of the new creation week, John's Gospel leads us to view Jesus and Mary in light of the Creation story. And it is in this context that Jesus calls Mary "woman." With the Genesis themes in the background, this title would bring to mind the "woman" of Genesis, Eve (Gen. 2:23, 3:20).

This woman played an important part in the first prophecy given to humanity. After the Fall, God confronted the serpent and announced his eventual defeat, saying:

> *I will put enmity between you and the woman,*
> *and between your seed and her seed;*
> *he shall bruise your head,*
> *and you shall bruise his heel.* (Gen. 3:15)

This statement, known as the *protoevangelium* ("first Gospel"), foretells that the woman one day will have a seed, a son, who will crush the head of the serpent.[*] Centuries later, at the

---

[*] *Catechism of the Catholic Church*, para. 410.

wedding feast of Cana, Jesus alludes to this prophecy. By calling Mary "woman" with the Creation story in the background, Jesus in the narrative of John's Gospel is associating Mary with the woman of Genesis 3:15. Far from rebuking his mother or distancing himself from her, Jesus, in calling Mary "woman," honors her in a way no woman ever had been honored before. She is the New Eve, the woman whose long-awaited son will defeat the devil and fulfill the prophecy of Genesis.

The Woman, the Hour, and the Wine

With this background in mind, we are prepared to understand the whole of Jesus's cryptic words to Mary at Cana: "Woman, what have you to do with me? My hour has not yet come" (John 2:4). There are three aspects of Jesus's words that need more delving into: "the hour"; the question ("what have you to do with me?"), and the unusual title given to Mary ("woman").

First, Jesus speaks about some mysterious "hour" of his and says it has not yet come. The "hour" of Jesus in the Gospel of John refers to the time appointed by the Father for Jesus to accomplish his mission. It ultimately points to the climax of his public ministry—his passion and death—when he is glorified, when the devil is defeated, and when Jesus gathers all people to himself (John 12:23–33, 13:1, 17:1). At Cana, Jesus associates Mary's request for wine with this hour of his passion, and he wonders why Mary is making this request since his hour has not yet come. His public ministry has not yet even begun.

Second, the idiomatic expression "what have you to do with me" (*ti emoi kai soi*) can be translated "what is this to me and to you?" In the Old Testament, the expression sometimes denotes hostility, conflict, or rebuke (Judg. 11:12; 2 Chron. 35:21; 1 Kings 17:18). Other times it expresses a lack of association or a difference of understanding—two people, for example, looking at something differently—but without the hostile overtones (2 Kings 3:13; Hosea 14:8). The shade of meaning depends on the context. Most view Jesus's use of this expression in John 2:4 as being along the lines of the second meaning, since a hostile tone does not fit with the way the Fourth Gospel presents Mary and Jesus's relationship at Cana.* At Cana, Mary implicitly asks Jesus to do something about the shortage of wine at the wedding feast, saying, "They have no wine." Jesus points out that he and Mary are looking at this request for wine with different eyes.

In the Jewish tradition, wine was a powerful symbol associated with Wisdom (Prov. 9:1–5; Sir. 17–21), with the Law, and with marriage feasts (Song of Sol. 1:2–4, 4:10, 5:1, 7:2). Most significant for this scene, wine was associated with *the joy of the messianic era*. The prophet Isaiah, for example, envisions all peoples gathering on the mountain of the Lord for a great feast of wine when God will come to save them (Isa. 25:6–9). The prophet Amos, similarly, foretells that when God restores the Davidic kingdom, "the mountains shall drip sweet wine, and all the hills shall flow with it" (Amos 9:13).

So when Jesus asks Mary, "What is this to me and to you?" it is as if he is saying to her, "What is this *wine* to me and to

---

*See the ecumenical work by Raymond Brown et al. *Mary in the New Testament: A Collaborative Assessment by Protestant and Roman Catholic Scholars* (New York: Paulist Press, 1978), 191; De la Potterie, *Mary in the Mystery of the Covenant*, 185.

you?"* For Mary, the wine she requests is simply a festive beverage that will help the families involved keep custom for the wedding celebration. But Jesus sees that in order to provide this wine, he will need to perform a miracle that will reveal his glory and launch the public ministry of his messianic mission. And this will begin his march toward the hour of his passion. Thus, from Jesus's perspective, Mary is asking for a lot more than a good supply of drink for the wedding feast. The wine she requests is really the messianic wine—the symbolic wine that the prophets foretold would accompany the messianic age. And as we have seen, Jesus associates Mary's request for this wine with his hour—the hour of his passion. Is Mary ready for that hour to arrive?

All this sheds additional light on why at this moment Jesus associates Mary with the "woman" of Genesis 3:15. If Jesus performs this miracle, he will start his messianic mission and thus initiate the march toward his hour. And if he does that, then Mary will assume a new role. Not only will she be Jesus's mother; Mary will become "woman"—the woman prophesied about in Genesis 3:15—in other words, the one whose son will defeat the devil.

---

*Ignace de la Potterie writes: "In other words, 'For me and for you, the word *wine* does not have the same meaning.' Scarcely having heard the word *wine*, Jesus thinks of the symbolism of wine in the biblical tradition" (*Mary in the Mystery of the Covenant*, 185).

Countdown to the Hour

So put yourself in Mary's shoes. At first, she is simply trying to help address the wine shortage at the wedding—not solve all the world's problems! She goes to Jesus with a basic request for wine and walks away confronted with much weightier matters involving her son's messianic mission, the defeat of the devil, and the solution to the problem of humanity's sin.

But even more: For thirty years, Mary has been carrying the burden of Simeon's prophecy. She knows that one day, once her son begins his ministry, he will be misunderstood, opposed, and rejected. She knows that her son is destined for "the fall and rising of many in Israel," and that he will be "a sign that is spoken against" (Luke 2:34). Ultimately, he will be killed: a sword will pierce him.

At the joyful occasion of a wedding feast, Mary simply asks Jesus for some wine. If Jesus heeds Mary's request, he will need to perform a miracle that will launch his public ministry—and that will formally initiate Jesus's movement toward the "hour" of his death. The clock on Simeon's prophecy will start clicking. Is this what Mary wants?

If we were the parent confronted with such a choice, many of us might pull back and say, "On second thought, Jesus, that's okay. You don't need to provide the wine after all!" But Mary does not cling to her son like that. How much of Jesus's profound statement Mary grasped right at that moment at Cana, the Gospel of John does not say. But however mysterious her son's words might have been for her, Mary shows no signs of hesitation. She learned when he was a twelve-year-old lost in the Temple that Jesus must be in his Father's house, doing the will of the Father, even if that means uncertainty, separation, and suffering for her. At Cana, therefore, Mary continues to say yes to God's will and to surrender to whatever he has planned for Jesus. She does not waver from the calling God has given her. She who is the servant of the Lord tells the servants at the feast, "Do whatever he tells you" (John 2:5). The servants obey. The miracle is performed. Christ's public ministry is launched. Mary, thus, helps set in motion the events that ultimately lead to her son's journey to Calvary, where he will die for our sins.

Total Surrender, Total Trust

———❈———

Standing by the Cross of Jesus (John 19:25–27)

At first glance one might conclude that Mary is not an important figure in the Gospel of John. She appears in only two scenes (at Cana and the cross), and she speaks only twice ("They have no wine" and "Do whatever he tells you"). Thus, a quantitative analysis would conclude that Mary is an insignificant character in John's Gospel.

But if one considers *when* she appears and what is specifically said about her, Mary's crucial role in this Gospel becomes clearer. Mary may appear only twice, but both scenes represent pivotal moments in Christ's life: the very beginning of his public ministry at Cana, and the climax of his mission as he is dying on the cross. In the initial event, Christ performed his first miracle and began to reveal his glory (John 2:11). In the latter event, Christ's glory is revealed most fully as he brings his redemptive mission to its culmination (see John 12:22–33). Mary has an important role to play in both of these critical scenes.

A second point: in both scenes Mary's presence is mentioned

three times, and each time she is not referred to by her personal name "Mary," but is identified by her relationship with Jesus as his "mother." These two details point to her intimate connection with her son.

A third link between Cana and the cross is the manner in which Jesus addresses Mary in both scenes. He doesn't call her "mother" or "Mary." Instead Jesus chooses a title that would have been highly unusual for a Jewish son to use when addressing his mother. He calls her "woman."

But the theme that most closely knits these two scenes together is John's reference to the mysterious "hour" of Jesus. At Cana, the theme of the hour was first introduced when Jesus told Mary, "My hour has not yet come" (John 2:4). At Calvary the mother is standing beside her son when the hour of his passion has arrived and his mission reaches its climax.

The Hour

The theme of Christ's "hour" runs as a narrative thread through the Gospel of John and creates dramatic suspense for us readers. We first encounter this motif at the beginning of Christ's public ministry during the wedding feast of Cana, when Jesus says to Mary, "My hour has not yet come" (John 2:4). At that point, Jesus does not clarify what this hour is or when it will come. He only says that this mysterious hour has yet to arrive.

Our curiosity intensifies as Jesus repeatedly refers to some supreme hour that is coming soon. For example, when addressing the Samaritan woman, he says that "the *hour* is coming . . . when the true worshipers will worship the Father in spirit and truth" (John 4:23). When addressing a crowd in Jerusalem, he says "the *hour* is coming . . . when the dead will hear the voice of the Son of God, and those who hear will live" (John 5:25).

Christ's cryptic hour is mentioned twice more in moments of intense conflict between Jesus and his opponents. But again, the nature and the timing of this hour remain veiled. When Jews in Jerusalem seek to arrest Jesus, John's Gospel notes that no one was able to lay hands on him "because his *hour* had not yet come" (John 7:30). Similarly, after a passionate debate with the Pharisees, no one was able to arrest Jesus "because his *hour* had not yet come" (8:20).

Over and over, we hear about this cryptic hour that is imminent. By the time we get halfway through John's Gospel, the average reader is left in much suspense! "What is this hour? And when will it ever come?"

The Hour Has Come

Thankfully, the long-awaited hour arrives at last in John 12. Just after he enters Jerusalem for what will be the last week of his life, Jesus announces that his hour is finally here: "*The hour has come* for the Son of man to be glorified" (John 12:23). And Jesus proceeds to tell us what his hour is all about: his sacrificial death on the cross, which brings about the defeat of the devil.

> "Now is the judgment of this world, *now shall the ruler of this world be cast out*; and I, when I am lifted up from the earth, will draw all men to myself." He said this to show by what death he was to die. (John 12:31–33)

Notice how Jesus speaks of his death not as a moment of defeat, but as a moment of victory. When he is lifted up on Calvary, the "ruler of this world"—the devil—will be cast out. This defeat of the devil recalls the famous prophecy of Genesis 3:15 in which God foretold that the woman would have a son who would crush the head of the serpent.

The Cross

Roman crucifixion was not just a form of execution. It was used to maximize a criminal's pain and public humiliation. The criminal was stripped naked and bound to a wooden cross with his arms extended, and then the cross was raised. Crucifixion did not aim at striking any vital organs or causing terminal bleeding. Rather, it was intended to bring about a slow and painful death through shock or asphyxiation as the unsupported body caused the breathing muscles to fatigue. Sometimes this could take a few days. Giving a criminal a footrest only enabled the victim to push himself up to breathe, thus prolonging the torture even more.

Sometimes a criminal was scourged before he was crucified. In a Roman scourging the prisoner was stripped and tied to a pillar or low post and then thrashed by a whip that had leather thongs with metal spikes or sharp pieces of bone attached to the ends; each time the victim was struck, his flesh would be torn open. As the skin was scourged repeatedly, the wounds were opened further, the muscles beneath torn into, and the bones exposed. Sometimes a scourging could cause death.

Soldiers had some control over how long a crucifixion would

last; a longer, severe scourging beforehand would weaken the prisoner and lead to a quick death on the cross. The fact that Jesus's crucifixion lasted only a few hours indicates that he experienced a very severe scourging.

Standing by the Cross

The New Testament does not tell us much about Mary's experience at Calvary. In fact, John's Gospel provides the only biblical record of her presence there. And it does not offer much of a picture. The mother of Jesus does not utter a single word, and her only action is to stand near her son's cross. Yet her "standing by the cross of Jesus" may tell us a lot about Mary as a faithful disciple.[*]

Ever since Jesus began speaking explicitly about his upcoming death in Jerusalem, he has been calling his disciples to share in his sufferings and follow him to the cross: "If any man would come after me, let him deny himself and take up his cross and follow me" (Matt. 16:24–28; cf. Mark 8:34–9:1; Luke 9:23–27). But most will fail Jesus on Good Friday by leaving him when he is taken away to be crucified. At the Last Supper, Jesus predicts that this is what will happen. He foretells how the apostles will abandon him: "The hour is coming, indeed it has come, when you will be scattered, every man to his home, and will leave me alone" (John 16:32).

Eleven out of the twelve apostles abandon Jesus on Good

---

[*] Beverly Gaventa, "Standing Near the Cross: Mary and the Crucifixion of Jesus," in *Blessed One: Protestant Perspectives on Mary,* ed. Beverly Gaventa and Cynthia Rigby (Louisville: Westminster John Knox Press, 2002), 49.

Friday. Only the beloved disciple, traditionally identified as John, perseveres with Jesus until the end. But four women stand at the cross of Jesus in his final moments. They exhibit much greater faithfulness than, for example, Peter, who said he wanted to follow Jesus wherever he went and even declared to Jesus, "I will lay down my life for you" (John 13:37). Yet faithfulness is proven not in words but in action. And Peter is not found *standing* at the cross of Jesus. Rather, when we see Peter "standing" in John's passion narrative, it is in the scene that depicts his greatest betrayal of Jesus. Peter "stood outside at the door" of the high priest during Jesus's trial (John 18:16), and then Peter was "standing and warming himself" around a fire when he denied Jesus three times (John 18:17–18, 25–27).

Mary is part of the group of women who prove to be more faithful and courageous than Peter and the other ten apostles who abandoned Jesus in his hour of greatest need. She is one of the few "standing by the cross of Jesus" on Good Friday. Moreover, John's Gospel also seems to indicate that Mary demonstrates faithfulness during the passion by sharing in her son's sufferings in a unique way.

The Woman in Labor

At the Last Supper, Jesus warns the apostles that the events that are about to unfold in his passion are not going to be easy for them. His disciples will endure intense suffering when Jesus is arrested, condemned, and crucified. But they also will rejoice when they are reunited with him after his resurrection. To make this point about the disciples' sorrow turning to joy, Jesus uses a striking analogy of a woman giving birth to a child.

A woman in labor experiences great travail, but she eventually rejoices once her child is delivered. Jesus says:

> Truly, truly, I say to you, you will weep and lament, but the world will rejoice; you will be sorrowful, but your sorrow will turn into joy. When a *woman* is in labor she has pain, because her *hour* has come; but when she is *delivered of the child*, she no longer remembers the anguish, for joy that a child is born into the world. So you have sorrow now, but I will see you again and your hearts will rejoice, and no one will take your joy from you. (John 16:20–22)

Jesus's disciples will be like a woman in labor: they will face great trauma when they are separated from Jesus at his death, but they will experience ecstatic joy when he rises from the dead.

Mary is presented in John's Gospel as a model disciple who exemplifies this sorrow turning to joy more than anyone else. As the mother of Jesus, she experiences the sorrow over the loss of him like no other. In fact, John's Gospel highlights how this allegory about the pains and joys of childbirth is concretely embodied in Mary's experience at the foot of the cross.

In the allegory, Jesus uses the image of *childbirth* to anticipate the *suffering Christ's disciples will face at his crucifixion.* He also uses two key words that have been employed earlier in John's Gospel in association with Mary at Cana: "woman" and "hour" (John 2:4). In this account of Jesus's farewell discourse at the Last Supper, Jesus speaks of a "woman" who gives birth in her "hour" (John 16:21). These same two themes (childbirth and Christ's death) and these same two key words ("woman" and "hour") are also linked with Mary in the scene at Calvary:

But standing by the cross of Jesus were his mother, and his mother's sister, Mary the wife of Clopas, and Mary Magdalene. When Jesus saw his *mother,* and the disciple whom he loved standing near, he said to his mother, "*Woman,* behold, your son!" Then he said to the disciple, "Behold, your *mother!*" And from that *hour* the disciple took her to his own home. (John 19:25–27)

The parallels between Jesus's birth analogy in John 16 and Mary's description at Calvary in John 19 are striking. Both involve a "woman" and the theme of the "hour." And both accounts use the image of motherhood and the theme of Christ's death. The numerous similarities underscore how the two scenes are meant to be read together. Mary at the cross embodies the birth pain parable from the Last Supper. She is the "woman" at the "hour" of Jesus's crucifixion. More than anyone else, Mary exemplifies the mother experiencing the metaphorical birth pains—the intense suffering of the faithful disciples who are separated from their Lord. As Catholic theologian Jean Galot commented,

More than all the others, Mary verified this picture of the woman who is about to give birth, because more than all the others she would be subject to grief at the time of the passion, and then filled with joy by the triumph of her son. . . . Mary fulfills in a unique way this figure which serves to describe the disciples' participation in the Passion.[*]

---

[*] Galot, *Mary in the Gospel,* 202.

Mary's Supreme Moment of Faith

Think about what this supreme moment of faith would have meant for Mary. John Paul II reflected on how contradictory the cross would have seemed, from a human perspective, to what Mary first heard from the angel at the Annunciation. At that time she was told that her son would "be great." God would give him the "throne of his father David." He would "reign over the house of Jacob for ever; and of his kingdom there would be no end" (Luke 1:32–33).

Now, standing at the foot of the cross, Mary witnesses what, to human eyes, appears to be "the complete *negation of these words*."* On Calvary, everything Gabriel announced to Mary about her son's everlasting kingdom seems to be proved wrong. According to John Paul II, only the most valiant faith could carry her through this darkest hour and enable her to remain a faithful disciple, standing by the cross of her son:

> How great, how heroic then is the obedience of faith shown by Mary in the face of God's "unsearchable judgments"! How completely she "abandons herself to God" without reserve, offering the full assent of the intellect and will to him whose "ways are inscrutable" (cf. Rom. 11:33)!†

Throughout her life Mary has been called to abandon herself to God's plan and to surrender to the mysteries unfolding before her. Her journey has led her through poverty and

---

* John Paul II, *Redemptoris Mater*, 18.
† Ibid., 18.

humiliation, and moments of uncertainty and incomprehension. But now it has taken her all the way to the Calvary where on Good Friday she witnesses not the glorious acceptance of her son as King, but his total rejection and torturous death. Here Mary faces her greatest test of faith. To human eyes, Christ does not look at all like a great king. Beaten, scourged, stripped, and nailed to a cross, Jesus looks more like a tragic failure being mocked and killed by his enemies. His crucifixion at the hands of the Romans and his enemies among his own people seems to mark the end to the Kingdom of God he was claiming he would build. But Mary is being challenged to see what John's Gospel emphasizes—that Jesus's crucifixion is actually his enthronement. When he is "lifted up" on the cross he is exalted as King, and "the ruler of this world"—the devil—is cast out (John 12:31–32).

At this crucial moment, however, no human crutch can support Mary. The only thing Mary can cling to is faith—faith that this is indeed the Son of God, who will reign forever; faith that she really is "the mother of my Lord" as Elizabeth told her; faith that this "sword" is truly part of God's plan as Simeon prophesied long ago, and that her son once again is doing his "Father's business." When Mary is found "standing by the cross of Jesus," she is, doubtless, experiencing great sorrow. But as a faithful disciple to the end, Mary also stands by the cross in great faith, trusting in God's plan for her son and clinging to what the Lord has revealed to her through angels, shepherds, prophets, and Jesus himself. John Paul II even teaches that Mary's faith at this moment would include belief in the words her son spoke to the disciples: that he "must go to Jerusalem and suffer many things from the elders and chief priests and scribes, and be killed, and on the third day be raised" (Matt. 16:21). Hence, John Paul II concludes that Mary's hope at the foot of the cross "contained a light stronger than the darkness that reigns in many hearts."*

The Mary of Good Friday

Mary's example on Good Friday offers us much hope in our own afflictions. There may be times when we face a trial so great that we may feel pushed to the edge in suffering and tempted to give up hope. The loss of a loved one, the loss of a job, the end of a relationship, a bewildering, painful dread that one's life is going nowhere. These are moments when we might desperately ask, "Why is this happening? How can I go on? Where is God in all this?" When our lives are utterly turned upside down, when the ground seems to be taken out from under us, when all is stripped away and there are no footholds, we come to know quite acutely how little control we really have over our lives— and how radically dependent we are on God.

It is then that we can stand with the Mary of Good Friday.

This is the Mary who witnessed the One who was the purpose of her life, the very reason for her existence, being taken from her in a cruel crucifixion. This is the Mary who from a human perspective witnessed the end of everything she had lived for. Yet she did not run away from this darkness nor did she fall into despair. She remained standing, with faith, at the

---

*John Paul II, General audience, April 2, 1947, in *Theotokos*, 184.

cross of Jesus. As Mother Teresa once wrote, "At the foot of the Cross, Our Lady saw only pain and suffering—and when they closed the tomb, she could not even see the Body of Jesus. But it was then that Our Lady's faith, her Loving Trust and Total Surrender were greatest."[*]

We, too, may have moments when we look at our lives and see "only pain and suffering." When facing trials, some people kick and scream and try everything in their power to change an unchangeable situation. Others just become hardened and bitter, blaming the world, blaming God, and lashing out at those around them. Still others might try to distract themselves from the hole in their hearts, filling their lives with constant activity, pursuits, entertainments, and pleasures—anything to cover up the emptiness and pain they feel deep within their souls.

But in the end, none of these coping mechanisms will work. Mary on Good Friday shows us the only healthy way forward: loving trust and total surrender. By her example she invites us to stand with her in that darkness and entrust ourselves to the only One who can carry us through. The Mary of Good Friday invites us to join her at the cross, to cling to God alone as she did, and to discover in a more profound way the strength that truly supports us not only in the most difficult times but at every moment of our lives.

[*] Mother Teresa to MC Sisters, March 14, 1997. Cited in Paul Murray, "The Silence of Mother Teresa," *Religious Life Review*, vol. 50 (May/June 2011): 146.

"Behold, Your Mother": Mary's New Mission

The account of Mary's presence at the cross also reveals a new mission that is entrusted to her. Jesus sees his mother and the beloved disciple there and he says to Mary, "Behold, your son," and to the disciple, "Behold, your mother" (John 19:26–27). On a basic level, Jesus's touching final words to Mary and his beloved disciple reveal Jesus's loving care for his mother. Just before he dies, Jesus thinks about how his mother will be cared for after his death, and he entrusts her to his closest disciple.

But there is something more. Since John's Gospel as a whole, and especially in its passion narrative, is filled with a lot of theological symbolism and concerned with the fulfillment of prophecy, it seems unlikely that these words are meant to convey merely Jesus's attention to Mary's material, human needs. Every detail of this particular scene at the cross points to God's plan coming to fulfillment. Consider the following examples.

First, just before Jesus addresses Mary and John from the cross, the Gospel mentions how the soldiers cast lots for Jesus's tunic and then goes on to explain that this was done to fulfill the Scriptures. The passage even quotes Psalm 22:18 to make the connection explicit: "They parted my garments among them, and for my clothing they cast lots" (John 19:24). Similarly, John 19:29 notes that the soldiers gave Jesus "a sponge full of the vinegar on hyssop and held it to his mouth," a direct allusion to Psalm 69:21: "and for my thirst they gave me vinegar to drink."

A third example: after Jesus dies, John goes out of his way to note that the soldiers did not break Jesus's legs—thus Jesus died like a sacrificial Passover lamb, whose bones were not to be broken (John 19:33; Exod. 12:46). Finally, John mentions that the soldier pierced Jesus's side (John 19:34), and he then quotes a prophecy from Zechariah: "They shall look on him whom they have pierced" (John 19:37; cf. Zech. 12:10).

Casting lots, vinegar to drink, bones left unbroken, pierced by a sword. In the Gospel of John these are not just bare historical facts. Every point is filled with a deeper level of symbolism and theological meaning. And right in the middle of this chorus of events announcing God's plan coming to fulfillment, Jesus says to Mary, "Woman, behold your son!" Given that the other details in this passage are charged with great significance, it seems most likely that there is something much more profound going on in John 19:25–27 than Jesus merely making sure someone looks after his mother after he dies.

The Beloved Disciple

One key to unlocking the deeper meaning of Jesus's giving his mother to his disciple and his disciple to his mother is to examine the role of the third major character mentioned in this account: the beloved disciple. Traditionally, the beloved disciple has been identified as the apostle John. Let us consider the important symbolic role this figure plays in the Fourth Gospel.

The Gospel of John often uses individual characters to symbolize larger groups. For example, in John 3, Nicodemus is described as "a man of the Pharisees" and a "ruler of the Jews" who comes to Jesus by night and does not understand Jesus's teachings (John 3:1). Some commentators note that Nicodemus represents the many Pharisees and other Jewish leaders who do not understand Christ and are left, like Nicodemus, in the dark. Similarly, the Samaritan woman in John 4 who has difficulty understanding Jesus's words but later comes to some level of faith represents the many Samaritans who have fallen away from Judaism but will come to believe in Christ.[*]

A closer look at the beloved disciple indicates that this figure represents more than an individual follower of Christ. He stands as the ideal disciple. The beloved disciple is the one who is close to Jesus, who leans on his master's breast at the Last Supper (John 13:25). He is the one apostle who remains with Jesus even in the face of Christ's suffering and persecution. The other apostles flee; only the beloved disciple follows Jesus all the way to the cross (John 19:26). The beloved disciple also is the first to believe in Christ's resurrection (John 20:8), and he is the first to bear witness to the risen Christ's Lordship (John 21:7).

Therefore, while the beloved disciple is traditionally identified as the individual apostle John, he also serves as a symbolic representative of all faithful disciples. The beloved disciple stands for all those who intimately follow Christ, even in the midst of the cross, and who believe in Jesus and bear witness to him as Lord. In other words, this individual disciple in the Gospel of John represents *all* beloved disciples of Jesus.

Mother of All Christians

In Jesus's last act before he dies, he entrusts this beloved disciple to his mother, to a filial relationship with Mary. On a deeper, spiritual level, since the beloved disciple represents all

---

[*]Craig Koester, *Symbolism in the Fourth Gospel: Meaning, Mystery, Community* (Minneapolis: Ausburg Fortress, 2003), 33–77.

faithful disciples, this passage has traditionally been interpreted as offering biblical support for the doctrine of Mary's spiritual motherhood over all Christians.[*] Mary is seen to be the mother of all the faithful followers of Jesus who are represented by the beloved disciple.

Reflecting on this passage, John Paul II explains that although Jesus does not explicitly spell out Mary's spiritual motherhood over all Christians, the passage does point us to this reality:

> Jesus's words, "Behold your son," effect what they express, making Mary the mother of John and of all the disciples destined to receive the gift of divine grace.
>
> On the cross Jesus did not proclaim Mary's universal motherhood formally, but established a concrete maternal relationship between her and the beloved disciple. In the Lord's choice we can see his concern that this motherhood should not be interpreted in a vague way, but should point to Mary's intense, personal relationship with individual Christians.
>
> May each one of us, precisely through the concrete reality of Mary's universal motherhood, fully acknowledge her as our own Mother, and trustingly commend ourselves to her maternal love.[†]

---

[*] Cf. *Catechism of the Catholic Church,* paras. 968–70.
[†] John Paul II, General audience, April 23, 1997, in *Theotokos,* 190.

Persevering in Faith

———— ❖ ————

Mary, Crowned with Glory (Revelation 12:1–17)

> And a great sign appeared in heaven, a woman
> clothed with the sun, with the moon under her feet,
> and on her head a crown of twelve stars. (Rev. 12:1)

Catholics throughout the centuries have often seen in this passage from the book of Revelation Mary's crowning moment. From the Annunciation to the cross, her pilgrimage of faith has taken her through many trials and ordeals, but at every step of the way she has proven to be a faithful servant of the Lord. She has "kept all these things, pondering them in her heart"—even when she did not understand. She has learned to conform her life more and more to her son's mission, which was to pursue his Father's affairs. And she did this even when the Father's plan caused her pain. As a result, she was not only Jesus's mother, but also a preeminent faithful disciple of his, following him all the way to the cross.

In the book of Revelation, Mary appears in heaven with royal splendor, "clothed with the sun" and crowned with twelve stars. Her journey with the Lord has led Mary to her ultimate destination. She has crossed the threshold into glory and shares in her son's heavenly reign as "Queen over all things," as the Catholic Church teaches.* Like Saint Paul, Mary could say, "I have fought the good fight, I have finished the race, I have kept the faith. From now on there is laid up for me the crown of righteousness, which the Lord, the righteous judge, will award to me on that Day, and not only me but also to all have loved his appearing" (2 Tim. 4:7–8).

The Catholic belief in Mary's queenship—her singular privilege of reigning with Christ over heaven and earth—should not be seen as something detached from our lives. Mary's royal magnificence is not something to be merely admired from afar as if it were completely removed from our own experience. Rather, her queenly position serves as an important reminder that all Christ's followers are called to share in his reign over sin and death. Mary thus stands as what the Church calls an "eschatological sign"—a sign pointing the way for Christians, revealing what God wants to accomplish in *all* our lives. Again, though Mary most fully shares in Christ's reign, she could say with Saint Paul that a "crown of righteousness" awaits not only her, but all who love Christ (see 2 Tim. 4:8).

But to understand this culminating step in Mary's pilgrimage of faith, we must see it as the fruition of all God has been doing in Mary's life. In this chapter we will step back and consider how the Bible reveals Mary as the first and model disciple, faithful from beginning to end. Then we will consider how the mysterious royal woman of chapter 12 of Revelation sheds light on Mary and her reward: the crown of righteousness.

---

* *Catechism of the Catholic Church*, para. 966.

Hearing God's Word and Doing It

Two of the most puzzling statements Jesus makes about Mary are found in Christ's public ministry. The Gospel of Luke reports that on one occasion, Mary comes to visit her son, and upon hearing that his mother wants to see him, Jesus responds in such a way that some readers might think that he is not that interested in seeing her:

> Then his mother and his brethren came to him, but they could not reach him for the crowd. And he was told, "Your mother and your brethren are standing outside, desiring to see you." But he said to them, "My mother and my brethren are those who hear the word of God and do it." (Luke 8:19–21)

At first glance this does not appear to be the warmest way to receive one's mother. Imagine, for example, if I were giving a lecture in Chicago and at the end of my presentation someone came into the room to tell me that my mother and siblings had arrived and were waiting outside to see me. Then, instead of joyfully welcoming them in, I said, "My mother and my brethren are those who hear the word of God and do it." Such a response would seem a little cold—and could even be viewed as a put-down of my family!

In another instance in Christ's public ministry an unnamed woman acknowledges Jesus's greatness and recognizes how blessed his mother must be: "A woman in the crowd raised her voice and said to him, 'Blessed is the womb that bore you, and the breasts that you sucked!'" (Luke 11:27). The woman's words praise Mary for being Jesus's mother according to the flesh. And Mary's maternal role is, indeed, worthy of praise. It is through her maternity that the Son of God became man, taking on human flesh—the flesh and blood of Mary. But Jesus does not seem comfortable with blessedness being understood as based *only* on natural family relations. He instead draws attention to all those who are faithful disciples, who obey God's word: "But he said, 'Blessed rather are those who hear the word of God and keep it!'" (Luke 11: 28).

What are we to make of these remarks about Mary? In both passages, when there is an opportunity to single out Mary for her honorable role as his mother, Jesus instead focuses on those who hear God's word and keep it—they are the ones who will be blessed (Luke 11:28) and who will be a part of a new spiritual family of disciples he is forming (Luke 8:21).

At the same time, Jesus's statements should not be seen as excluding Mary from those counted as "blessed" in Christ's kingdom, nor should Jesus be seen as distancing himself from his mother. Rather, both instances point to a new kind of relationship he has with Mary as his public ministry emerges. As John Paul II explained, Jesus "wishes to divert attention from motherhood understood only as a fleshly bond, in order to direct it towards those mysterious bonds of the spirit which develop from hearing and keeping God's word."*

We have seen that when the twelve-year-old Jesus is found in the Temple, his supreme allegiance to doing his heavenly Father's will takes precedence over all human relationships and

---

*John Paul II, *Redemptoris Mater,* 20.

worldly considerations: "Did you not know I must be in my Father's house?" (Luke 2:49). Now in his public ministry of proclaiming the Kingdom of God, Jesus's fulfillment of his Father's will adds a new dimension to all human relationships. All must be centered on doing the Father's work. Mary may have said yes to being mother of the Messiah back at the Annunciation, but now in Jesus's proclamation of the Kingdom, she—along with the rest of Israel—is being invited to be a part of the spiritual family of disciples Jesus is forming. The two criteria Jesus sets for being blessed in his kingdom and belonging to his spiritual family are hearing God's word and obeying it.

First Disciple

And Mary meets these criteria more than anyone else in Luke's Gospel. In fact, she is the first in Luke's Gospel to hear the word of God and keep it. John Paul II wrote: "Thus *in a sense* Mary as Mother became *the first 'disciple' of her son,* the first to whom he seemed to say: 'Follow me,' even before he addressed this call to the Apostles or to anyone else (cf. Jn. 1:43 [emphasis added])."*
At the Annunciation, she hears the word of God through the angel and responds to it with her "fiat." She describes herself as a servant of the Lord and joyfully surrenders herself to God's plan for her, saying, "Let it be [done] to me according to your word" (Luke 1:38).

Moreover, Mary continued to "hear" and "keep" God's word all throughout her life. We see Mary's obedience to God's word

---

*John Paul II, *Redemptoris Mater,* 21.

in the Visitation scene in two ways. First, Mary hears the angel's message about Elizabeth's miraculous pregnancy, believes it, and goes in haste to visit her (1:36, 39). Second, Elizabeth specifically praises Mary as someone who is blessed because she believes—"blessed is she who believed that there would be a fulfillment of what was spoken to her from the Lord" (Luke 1:45). Mary thus is counted in Luke's Gospel among the "blessed" who hear and keep God's word.

We see Mary's obedience to God's word also in the naming of the Christ child. Luke notes how Mary obeys the angel's instruction to name the child Jesus: the child "was called Jesus, the name given by the angel before he was conceived in the womb" (Luke 2:21). Furthermore, when Mary hears of the angelic revelation given to the shepherds about her son, and when she hears Jesus's cryptic words about needing to be in his "Father's house," she "kept all these things, pondering them in her heart" (Luke 2:19, cf. 2:51). Again, Mary is a faithful disciple who hears the word of God and strives to keep it.

Mary's faithfulness continues into Christ's adulthood and public ministry. At Cana she instructs others to listen to her son's word and obey it, saying, "Do whatever he tells you" (John 2:5). She perseveres in her walk with the Lord all the way to the end, when she is among the few found "standing by the cross of Jesus" in his dying moments on Calvary. Finally, Mary is singled out in the early Church as the only person named among the faithful disciples praying with the apostles in Jerusalem as they await the coming of the Holy Spirit (Acts 1:14).

The Woman Clothed with the Sun

All throughout her life—from the Annunciation to just before Pentecost—Mary is presented in the New Testament as a faithful disciple who heard the word of God and kept it. Since Mary is the first and model disciple, it is not surprising that she would be depicted as sharing in the rewards of Christ's kingdom in a preeminent way. A passage from chapter 12 of the book of Revelation reveals the mother of the Messiah in this way, full of royal magnificence:

> And a great portent appeared in heaven, a woman clothed with the sun, with the moon under her feet, and on her head a crown of twelve stars; she was with child and she cried out in her pangs of birth, in anguish for delivery. And another sign appeared in heaven; behold, a great red dragon, with seven heads and ten horns, and seven diadems upon his heads. . . . And the dragon stood before the woman who was about to bear a child, that he might devour her child when she brought it forth; she brought forth a male child, one who is to rule all the nations with a rod of iron, but her child was caught up to God and to his throne. (Rev. 12:1–5)

In the Catholic tradition the woman in this passage has often been connected with Mary. But many have interpreted the woman as not having Marian significance; they see her instead as a symbol of Israel or the Church. To properly identify this mysterious woman, we must consider the three main characters in this scene: the woman, her male child, and the dragon. The woman gives birth to the male child, who is attacked by the dragon. The child is caught up to God and enthroned while the dragon is defeated and cast down (Rev. 12:1–9).

Two of the three characters are easily identifiable. The *dragon* is explicitly identified in verse 9 as "that ancient serpent, who is called the Devil and Satan" (Rev. 12:9). The *male child* is Jesus, for he is described as "one who is to rule all the nations with a rod of iron" (Rev. 12:5)—a reference to the description of the messianic king in Psalm 2:6–9. Furthermore, since the child is caught up to God and sits on his throne, most scholars identify the child as Christ.

The Third Character

The identity of the "woman" is not as explicit. To identify the woman we must consider five key facts we learn about her in Revelation 12.

First, the woman has a crown of twelve stars, which recalls the twelve apostles and the twelve tribes of Israel.

Second, she delivers her child with birth pains.* This recalls the Daughter Zion prophecies of the Old Testament. Zion is the mountain of Jerusalem that is personified as a mother figure who endures labor pains before giving birth to a child. The

---

*If the woman described in Revelation 12 as "[crying] out in her pangs of birth, in anguish for delivery" is associated with Mary, this would not necessarily be opposed to the traditional Catholic belief that Mary, who remained a virgin while giving birth to Jesus, did not experience birth pains. John's Gospel uses birth pain imagery to describe not a physical birth, but Christ's death and resurrection (John 16:20–21). Similarly, the book of Revelation uses birth imagery to describe Christ's resurrection, his being the "firstborn of the dead" (Rev. 1:5). Thus, Revelation 12 is likely drawing our attention not as much to Jesus's birth in Bethlehem, as to the metaphorical birth of his death and resurrection.

image of lady Zion giving birth became a powerful symbol for how the faithful Jewish people would endure many sufferings in the period leading up to the messianic age (e.g., Isa. 26:17–19, 66:7–8).

Third, the woman gives birth to the Messiah, the one who "is to rule all the nations with a rod of iron" (Rev. 12:5; cf. Ps. 2:9).

Fourth, the woman's son fulfills what the Lord says in Genesis 3:15, foretelling that the woman would have a descendant who would defeat the devil. Chapter 12 of Revelation dramatically depicts the fulfillment of this prophecy as the dragon (Satan) is cast down to earth and defeated while the woman's male child is "caught up to God and to his throne" (Rev. 12:5–9).

Fifth, the woman experiences the blessings of a new exodus. After her son's victory over the devil, the woman flees to the wilderness, where she is nourished by God and rescued by eagle's wings (Rev. 12:6, 13–16)—images that recall the Exodus story, in which Israel was brought out into the wilderness, where she was nourished by God with the manna (Exod. 16:4–5) and protected by eagle's wings, as God says to them, "You have seen what I did to the Egyptians, and how I bore you on eagles' wings and brought you to myself" (Exod. 19:4).

Is There Room for Mary?

With this background we can understand why the "woman" is seen by some as a symbol for the Church. Like the Church, the woman in Revelation 12 is protected and nourished by God; the imagery in Revelation 12:13–16 describes God protecting his people in the new covenant age.

We also can appreciate why others interpret the "woman" as a symbol for the Old Testament people of God, Israel. This view makes sense out of the woman's crown of twelve stars, which recalls the twelve tribes of Israel. It also explains the birth pain image, which recalls the Daughter Zion prophecies about the trials God's people would face.

Is there room for seeing Mary in this scene? While the "woman" still may have some symbolic meaning pointing to Israel or the Church, we must keep in mind that she is portrayed as the mother of the Messiah. And wouldn't a reference to the Messiah's mother bring to mind Mary? It seems quite unlikely that the earliest Christians would not have seen Mary *at all* in this woman. As Scripture scholar André Feuillet asks, "Is it conceivable that a Christian author of the late first century could speak about the Mother of Christ while prescinding entirely from the Virgin Mary?"[*] Moreover, since the other two main characters in the passage are identified as individuals (the male child = Jesus; the dragon = Satan), it seems unlikely that the third major character, the woman, is not an individual at all, but *only* a symbol for a collective group. Rather, if the dragon and the child represent individuals, the woman is likely to represent an individual as well.

Furthermore, given the biblical notion of individuals representing larger groups of people (a topic we briefly considered with the "beloved disciple" in the previous chapter),[†] the woman

---

[*] André Feuillet, *Jesus and His Mother: The Role of the Virgin Mary in Salvation History and the Place of Woman in Church,* trans. Leonard Maluf, Studies in Scripture (Still River, Mass.: St. Bede's Publications, 1984), 23.

[†] See also, for example, Rom. 5:12–19, where Adam represents all humanity and Ps. 44:4, where the individual Jacob stands for all of Israel.

in Revelation 12 could be understood to be *both* an individual (Mary) *and* a representative of God's people as a whole (Israel and/or the Church). And Mary would be just the right person to embody both the old and the new covenant people since she herself stands at the hinge between the old and the new. If there was one woman in salvation history who could best represent both old covenant Israel and the beginning of the new covenant people of God, it would certainly be Mary.

The Same Woman: Mary in John 19

But there is still one more argument that makes the Marian interpretation of the woman in Revelation 12 even clearer.

In John 19, we see from an earthly perspective what happens on Calvary: Jesus is crucified by the Romans while his mother and the beloved disciple stand at the foot of the cross. Revelation 12 portrays the same scene, but from a heavenly perspective, so that we can see with the eyes of angels what really happens on Good Friday: Calvary is the climactic cosmic showdown between God and the devil, and the real force behind Christ's crucifixion is not the Romans or the Jewish leaders in Jerusalem but Satan. While John 19 presents soldiers crucifying Jesus on the cross, Revelation 12 shows us the dragon fiercely attacking the woman's son (Rev. 12:4–5), and the son emerging victorious, being enthroned in heaven while the devil is defeated and cast down (Rev. 12:7–9).

In the midst of this ultimate battle stands the "woman" in both scenes. There are four key parallels between the way the woman in Revelation 12 is portrayed and the way Mary at the cross in John 19 is described, and together these elements highlight the connection between the woman in Revelation and Mary.

(1) "Woman": Just as Revelation 12:1 presents a figure that is called "a woman" and who is described in such a way that she is shown to be the mother of the Messiah (12:5), so Mary in John 19:25–27 is called "woman" and stands at the cross as the mother of the king.

(2) Birth Pains: Both women are portrayed in scenes involving the Daughter Zion birth pain theme. This is explicit with the woman in Revelation 12:1–2, but the scene of Mary at the cross in John 19 also has birth pain imagery linked to the allegory Jesus tells at the Last Supper in John 16:20–21.

> When a *woman* is in labor, she has pain, because her *hour* has come; but when she is delivered of the child, she no longer remembers the anguish, for joy that a child is born into the world. So you have sorrow now, but I will see you again and your hearts will rejoice, and no one will take your joy from you. (John 16:20–22 [emphasis added])

In the allegory, the "woman" in her "hour" foreshadows the scene of Christ's passion and death. This symbolism stands in the background of the scene of Mary at the cross—a scene that similarly involves Mary being called "woman" (John 19:26) at the very hour of Christ's passion (cf. Rev. 12:27–31).

(3) Satan's Defeat: Third, just as the woman in Revelation 12 gives birth to a male child who rises up victoriously to a throne in heaven while the devil is conquered and thrown out (Rev. 12:5–9), so Mary in John 19 stands at the cross with her

messianic son in his "hour"—which John's Gospel portrays as the victorious hour when he is lifted up on the cross and the devil is cast down (John 12:27–31).

(4) Twofold Maternity: Fourth, both women are described as the mother of Jesus and as having a special motherly relationship with all of Christ's faithful followers. The woman in Revelation 12 is the mother not only of the individual Messiah (Rev. 12:5), but also of Christians "who keep the commandments of God and bear testimony to Jesus" (Rev. 12:17); whereas Mary at the cross is presented not only as Jesus's mother (John 19:25–26), but also as the mother of the beloved disciple—a figure who represents all faithful disciples (as we have discussed in a previous chapter).

All these parallels between the woman in Revelation 12 and Mary in John 19—"woman," birth pains, Satan's defeat, the mother of Christ, and the mother of Christ's followers—show a unity of thought about the woman figure in John's writings. Therefore, if the woman in John 19 is clearly understood to be Mary, the woman in Revelation 12 also should be seen as Mary.

Crowned with Glory

Once the woman in Revelation 12 is identified as Mary, we can see how this passage reveals where Mary's journey with God ultimately leads her: to be crowned with glory in heaven and to share in Christ's reign, a promise he makes to all his faithful disciples.

Revelation 12 introduces Mary as a majestic queenly figure, reflecting her exalted royal status:

> And a great sign appeared in heaven, a woman clothed with the sun, with the moon under her feet, and on her head a crown of twelve stars. (Rev. 12:1)

This verse reveals Mary's royal splendor in three ways. First, she wears a *crown,* symbolizing her royal status in heaven. Second, the woman having "the moon under her feet" also points to her royalty, for in the Bible, having something under one's foot depicts royal dominion and victory over one's enemies (e.g., Ps. 110:1). Third, the triple celestial image of the woman being clothed with the *sun,* with the *moon* under her feet, and crowned with twelve *stars* also demonstrates her royal authority. Similar imagery is found in the patriarch Joseph's dream in which the sun, moon, and eleven stars bow down before him, symbolizing the royal authority that the patriarch Joseph would have over his father and mother (symbolized by the *sun* and *moon*) and over his brothers (represented by eleven *stars*). Revelation 12 depicts Mary with these same three celestial images, thus demonstrating a royal authority reminiscent of Joseph's.

In this last book of the Bible, therefore, Mary appears in heaven, in royal splendor, participating in her son's victorious kingdom. This is the consequence of her constant faithfulness throughout her life—from the Annunciation to her gathering with the Church in prayer before Pentecost. She is awarded the crown of righteousness and a share in her son's reign. But as we noted at the outset of this chapter, her royal status should not be seen as disconnected from the walk of every Christian disciple. Her queenship is not meant to be admired from afar; her royal way of faithfulness and service to the Lord is to be imitated within the soul of every believer.

The New Testament teaches that all of Christ's faithful followers will share in his reign. Jesus, for example, told the apostles that everyone who has been willing to give up everything and follow him will "sit on thrones, judging the twelve tribes of Israel" (Matt. 19:28–30). Similarly, he promised that his disciples who persevere with him through his trials will rule over the new Israel (Luke 22:28–30). Saint Paul reflects this teaching, pointing out to Timothy, "If we have died with him, we shall also live with him; if we endure, we shall also reign with him (2 Tim. 2:11–12). In the book of Revelation, Mary is not the only person who is offered a crown. The image of a crown refers to the share in Christ's kingship that is given to all the saints as a reward for their perseverance in faith through trials, temptation, and persecution (Rev. 2:10; 3:11; 4:4, 10; 6:2; 14:14). Since the New Testament reveals Mary as a model disciple of Jesus, someone who hears the word of God and keeps it (Luke 1:38, 45; 8:21; 11:28), and someone who remains faithful throughout her life (Acts 1:14), and even perseveres with him through his death on the cross (John 19:25–27; cf. Luke 2:34–35), it is most fitting that the book of Revelation depicts her in royal glory, sharing in Christ's reign with a crown of twelve stars on her head.

With this background, we can see that Mary crowned with glory stands as a constant reminder—an "eschatological sign"—of what God wants to accomplish in all our lives. If we are faithful disciples like Mary, if we persevere in our walk of faith and use our lives to serve God's plan, we, too, will share in Christ's glorious reign. But as our Queen Mother (see Step 3), she also guides us on our own pilgrimage of faith through her prayers. Mary constantly intercedes for us in heaven that we might be more deeply united to her son and that we might, like Saint Paul, fight the good fight, finish the race, and join her in her son's heavenly kingdom. As a woman who has made her own pilgrimage of faith through various discernments, uncertainties, trials, and adversities, she remains very close to her spiritual children on earth both in her understanding of the human experience and in her loving intercession for us. As John Paul II explains,

> Thus far from creating distance between her and us, Mary's glorious state brings about a continuous and caring closeness. She knows everything that happens in our lives and supports us with maternal love in life's trials.
>
> Taken up into heavenly glory, Mary dedicates herself totally to the work of salvation in order to communicate to every living person the happiness granted to her. She is a queen who gives all that she possesses, participating above all in the life and love of Christ.[*]

---

[*] Pope John Paul II, General audience, July 23, 1997 in *Theotokos*, 211–12.

Her Last Words

————— ✳ —————

Walking with Mary Today

M ary's command to the servants at the Wedding at
Cana—"Do whatever he tells you" (John 2:5)—are her
last recorded words in the Bible. And they are like a last will
and testament to all of us who wish to follow Christ. Through
these words, Mary exhorts us to trust Jesus completely just as
she abandoned herself to God's plan step-by-step throughout
her life as the humble servant of the Lord.

First, Mary's words to the servants at the Wedding at Cana
are typical of the obedient response given by God's people living under the covenant of the Old Testament. For example,
the theme of doing "whatever he tells you" appears three times
when Israel established its covenant with Yahweh at Mount
Sinai. When Moses first announces to the Israelites their mission and duties as God's chosen people, the whole congregation responds, "All that the Lord has spoken we will do" (Exod.
19:8). And when God establishes this covenant with Israel in a

ritual ceremony at Sinai, Moses solemnly announces the words of the Lord to the people, and the congregation twice again responds, "All the words which the Lord has spoken we will do" (Exod. 24:3, 7).

Similar words were repeated later in Israel's history when the people renew their covenant as they settled in the Promised Land (Josh. 24:24), and later when they begin to rebuild Jerusalem after their exile in Babylon (Neh. 5:12). Thus, at the pivotal moments in Israel's history—the covenant at Sinai, entering the Promised Land, and at the restoration of Jerusalem—doing whatever God says is paramount and is closely associated with covenant obedience.

This sheds light on Mary's words at the wedding feast of Cana. At the dawn of the messianic era, another turning point in Israel's history has arrived. As the Messiah is about to perform his first miracle and thereby launch his public ministry, we once again encounter the theme of doing whatever God says. Mary tells the servants, "Do whatever he tells you," and with these words, she echoes the profession of faith of Israel at Sinai. Mary "personifies in a certain manner the people of Israel in the context of the covenant" and stands as a faithful representative of Israel.[*]

Joseph and Jesus

Second, Mary's words find a close parallel with what Pharaoh said about Joseph in the book of Genesis. During the severe

---

[*] De la Potterie, *Mary in the Mystery of the Covenant,* 190. See also A. Serra, "Bibbia," in *Nuovo Dizionario di Mariologia,* ed. S. De Fiores and S. Meo (Milano: Edizioni San Paolo, 1986), 253.

famine in Egypt, Pharaoh puts Joseph in charge of storing up the wheat harvest in the plentiful years before the famine and distributing it once the food crisis arrived. When the starving people cry for provisions, Pharaoh tells them, "Go to Joseph; what he says to you, do" (Gen. 41:55)—an expression that's almost identical to what Mary would later say at Cana.

This biblical connection between doing whatever Joseph says and doing whatever Jesus says is quite significant, for there are several parallels between Joseph and Jesus in these two scenes. Just as Joseph overcomes a lack of food during the famine with his storehouses of grain, so Jesus overcomes a lack of wine at the wedding by changing a large volume of water into wine. Just as Joseph is presented as having the Spirit of God in him at the beginning of his work (Gen. 41:38), so Jesus is described as having the Spirit upon him at the start of his ministry (John 1:32). Just as Joseph is thirty years old when he begins to store up the grain for the people (Gen. 41:46), so Jesus is thirty years old when he provides the wine for people at the wedding feast (cf. Luke 3:23). And just as Pharaoh's words about Joseph—"what he says to you, do"—come when Joseph steps into his leadership role in Egypt, so Mary's words—"do whatever he tells you"—come when Jesus begins his public ministry by performing the first miracle in his kingly mission.

Trust Without Hesitation

Finally, let's consider how Mary's command "Do whatever he tells you" has profound effects on the servants, inspiring them to trust Jesus in a radical way. Just put yourself in the servants' shoes. Jesus tells them to take the six stone jars for the Jewish rites of purification, fill them up with water, and draw some out to present to the steward of the feast. These stone jars would have been used for the ritual washing of hands. Astonishingly, Jesus tells the servants to fill up these very jars with water and then present this water to their boss so that the contents can be served to the guests.

This would take a lot of faith! Imagine what the servants are thinking: "Fill up *these* jars? With *water*? And serve it to the guests? How is *this* going to solve the problem?" From a merely human perspective, Jesus's plan does not make any sense. Yet, first and foremost, Jesus is asking the servants not to understand his plan but to trust him.

And they do trust him. John's Gospel highlights that the servants respond as faithful disciples, promptly following Christ's commands, no matter how mysterious those commands might appear to them. Jesus gives two orders to the servants. First, he tells them, "Fill the jars with water," and John's Gospel immediately points out that the servants not only obey Christ's command, but they do so perfectly: "And they filled them up *to the brim*" (John 2:7). Second, Jesus tells them, "Now draw some out, and take it to the steward of the feast," and John's Gospel notes, "So they took it" (John 2:8). Notice how John's Gospel goes out of its way to tell us that the servants do exactly as they are told.

Jesus	*The Servants*
"*Fill* the jars"	"And they *filled* them" (John 2:7)
"*Take* it to the steward"	"So they *took* it" (John 2:8)

Clearly, these servants followed Mary's exhortation, "Do whatever he tells you." They are faithful disciples, obedient to Christ's words. Significantly, John's Gospel presents them not as mere slaves, but as servants in the sense of disciples. Instead of using the Greek word for slaves, *doulois,* John's Gospel describes these men as servants, *diakonois,* a Greek word that in John refers to the true disciples of Jesus. For example, in John 12:26, Jesus speaks of his faithful disciples when he says, "If any one serves [*diakonei*] me, he must follow me; and where I am, there shall my servant [*diakonos*] be also." Thus we can see that Mary's command "Do whatever he tells you" has a powerful impact. Mary stirs the servants to respond like model disciples, giving prompt obedience to Jesus.[*]

And her last words at Cana are meant to encourage us today. We are called to be like the servants at the feast, completely trusting God with our lives and giving perfect obedience to Christ as they did. We, too, may not always grasp Jesus's work in our lives. We may not see clearly where the Lord is leading us. Yet, as John Paul II reminds us,

> Mary's request "Do whatever he tells you," is an exhortation to trust without hesitation, especially when one does not understand the meaning or benefit of what Christ asks.[†]

---

[*] See De la Potterie, *Mary in the Mystery of the Covenant,* 190.

[†] John Paul II, General audience, February 26, 1997, in *Theotokos,* 175.

Words Born from Experience

With this background we can see how Mary's words "Do whatever he tells you" should inspire us to tremendous faith. Indeed, this is not a legalistic command to obey or just a catchy spiritual slogan. These are confident words *born from experience.* All throughout her life, from Nazareth to the cross, Mary has lived by this principle of obedience. She has learned to surrender herself to whatever the Lord may be asking of her. She has learned what it means to walk with God.

Recall how she trusted without hesitation the Lord's call when the angel appeared to her in Nazareth. That initial faith was put to the test several times as she kept and pondered the mystery of her son's poverty, humility, and rejection at his birth; as she reflected on Simeon's stark words about the sword; and as she experienced her own lack of understanding about why Jesus was lost to her for three days in the Temple. In this sense, Mary did not have just one annunciation and one definitive "fiat." At each moment in her life, whether she experienced rejoicing, friendship, and clarity or suffering, darkness, and the cross, Mary was given many opportunities to reaffirm her initial "yes" to God in Nazareth.

Now, after traveling so far in her pilgrimage of faith, Mary, with a holy confidence, exhorts us to live out what has served as the foundational principle for her own existence: "Do whatever he tells you." For it is only when we walk in Mary's footsteps as faithful disciples, doing the Lord's bidding, that we will find, as Mary did, the happiness and fulfillment Christ has in store for all his followers and the crown of glory awaiting us in heaven.

About the Author

DR. EDWARD SRI is a nationally known Catholic author and speaker and frequent guest on EWTN. He has written several Catholic bestselling books, including *A Biblical Walk Through the Mass: Understanding What We Say and Do in the Liturgy* (Ascension); *The New Rosary in Scripture: Biblical Insights for Praying the 20 Mysteries* (Servant); and *Men, Women, and the Mystery of Love: Practical Insights from John Paul II's Love and Responsibility* (Servant).

Edward is the creator and host of the Augustine Institute's new video resource for Catholic parishes called *Symbolon Adult Faith Formation* and *Symbolon RCIA.* He is a founding leader with Curtis Martin of FOCUS (Fellowship of Catholic University Students) and the general editor of *Opening the Word*, a journey through the Sunday Mass readings. He currently serves as vice president of mission and outreach and as a professor of theology and scripture at the Augustine Institute master's program in Denver, Colorado, and enjoys leading pilgrimages to

Rome for laypeople each year. Edward holds a doctorate from the Pontifical University of St. Thomas Aquinas in Rome. He resides with his wife, Elizabeth, and their six children in Littleton, Colorado. To learn more about Edward Sri, visit www.AugustineInstitute.org.

QUESTIONS FOR REFLECTION
AND DISCUSSION

Step 1: An Open Heart

- At every Mass, Catholics hear the greeting "The Lord be with you"—an echo of the words Gabriel spoke to Mary. How were those words used in the Old Testament Scriptures? What did the greeting indicate for Mary? And what might those words mean for us today when we hear them in the Mass?

- Mary "considered in her mind" the angel's greeting. We observe that this expression describes how Mary remained in dialogue with God's word, open to whatever God might be calling her to do. How do you typically respond when you sense God might be asking you to do something difficult, make a change, or give up something you like? How does Mary model for us the proper disposition we should always have before God?

- We have learned how Mary found favor with God, which means that God viewed her as someone to whom he could entrust a lot. Consider a responsibility or person God has entrusted to your care. Do you think God looks on you with favor in what he has entrusted to you? Why or why not?

Step 2: A Servant of the Lord

- Mary described herself as a "servant of the Lord." Does this idea of being God's servant—being totally at the disposal of God's plans for you—seem exciting or frightening? Why?

- What is one area in your life where you can give up your own interests, desires, and pursuits more in order to be free to serve God and others more?

- Mary didn't just do God's will. She did it joyfully, like a lover wanting to fulfill the desires of her beloved. Describe something in your life now that you wish you could do more joyfully, like Mary.

Step 3: Magnify the Lord

- When you feel busy and have a lot to do, how attentive are you to others' needs? How might Mary's example in the Visitation scene inspire you to consider others more when you feel overwhelmed in life?

- Mary, in her prayer known as the Magnificat, models true humility. We learn how she comes to understand what Jesus would later teach: "Without me you can do nothing." If someone observed your life from the outside, would they conclude that you were someone who lived as if they were completely dependent on God? Or would they see someone who trusted more in their own planning, talent, and effort?

- Mary praises the Lord for the great things he has done for her. What is something God has done for you for which you can give him praise and thanks?

Step 4: Keep and Ponder
- How do you respond when you feel you are not treated well or things don't go your way?
- We have considered how Mary responds to the difficult, humble circumstances surrounding her son's birth by keeping all these things and pondering them in her heart. What does this expression—to keep and ponder in one's heart—mean?
- What, practically, can you do to be more like Mary the next time you face difficulty, humiliation, or suffering?

Step 5: Sharing in the Sword
- Mary and Joseph are introduced in this scene as model, faithful Jews, careful to be obedient to the law. How might their example inspire you? Is there an area in your life where you need to be more attentive in following God's law?
- Forty days after Jesus was born, Mary heard this ominous prophecy about her son's future rejection and death. What do you think it would be like for Mary to carry the burden of such a prophecy from the time of Jesus's infancy and childhood through his adulthood and public ministry?
- In this chapter, we saw how Mother Teresa encouraged her sisters not to run away from suffering, describing it

as an opportunity to draw nearer to Jesus in his suffering. How do you feel about this call to share in Christ's suffering?

Step 6: Walking in Darkness

- How do you think Mary felt when she realized her child was missing? How do you think she might have responded *spiritually* to this crisis? What do you think she would have been saying to God in those hours?

- In times when you feel Jesus is lost to you, how might Mary's experience of losing her son in Jerusalem be comforting for you?

- And when we experience darkness, how might Jesus's words to Mary—"Did you not know I must be about my Father's house?"—shed light on what Jesus may be doing?

Step 7: She Still Says Yes

- At Cana, Mary is a model of compassion as she notices the crisis at hand and turns to Jesus with the problem. How well do you notice the needs of the people in your life—your family, coworkers, friends? How might Mary's example inspire you to be more attentive to others' needs?

- Mary at Cana is a loving intercessor, looking upon the needs of the wedding couple with compassion and bringing the problem to her son. How comfortable are you turning to Mary as an intercessor?

- Mary tells the servants at the wedding feast to obey Jesus's commands: "Do whatever he tells you." What do you think Jesus might be telling you to do in your life now?

Step 8: Total Surrender, Total Trust

- How might Mary's example of total trust and surrender at the cross encourage us in our own moments of suffering?

- In this chapter, we considered how Jesus gives his mother to us as our spiritual mother. Imagine Jesus on Calvary looking you in the eyes and saying what he told the beloved disciple: "Behold your mother." Are you willing to accept Jesus's gift to us of his own mother?

- What do you think it means to welcome Mary and have a relationship with her as your spiritual mother?

Step 9: Persevering in Faith

- Mary is rewarded for her continuous faithfulness all throughout her life. She is crowned with twelve stars on her head (Rev. 12:1). How might Mary's crowning in heaven encourage you to persevere in your own walk with the Lord?

- Mary is also revealed as the mother of all who "keep the commandments of God and bear testimony to Jesus" (Rev. 12:17)—in other words, as mother of all faithful Christians. How might you explain to a friend the blessings of having Mary as spiritual mother?

- After reading this book, what is the biggest insight you gained about Mary? In what ways have you been inspired to follow her example more? In what ways might you be drawn to develop a deeper relationship with her?

"Must-reading for anyone who has ever wanted to know who the
Virgin Mary really was and what her life means for us today."
—DR. BRANT PITRE, author of *Jesus and the Jewish Roots of the Eucharist*

Mary appears only a few times in the Bible, but those few passages come at crucial moments. Catholics believe that Mary is the ever-virgin Mother of God,
the Queen of Heaven and Earth. But she was also a human being—a woman
who made a journey of faith through various trials and uncertainties, and who
endured her share of suffering. Even with her unique graces and vocation, Mary
remains a woman we can relate to and from whom we have much to learn.

In *Walking with Mary,* Edward Sri looks at the key passages in the Bible concerning Mary and offers insight into the Blessed Mother's faith and devotion that
we can apply to our daily lives. We follow her step-by-step through the New
Testament account of her life, reflecting on what the Scriptures tell us about how
she responded to the dramatic events unfolding around her.

Drawing on the wisdom of sacred Scripture and Catholic tradition, Sri's highly
readable and accessible book is a call to action for all of us to walk in the footsteps of
the Mother of Mercy as we make our own pilgrimage of faith in our day-to-day life.

DR. EDWARD SRI is an internationally
known Catholic speaker who appears regularly
on EWTN and is the author of several well-
loved Catholic books. He is a founding leader,
with Curtis Martin, of FOCUS (Fellowship of
Catholic University Students), and professor of
theology and scripture at the Augustine Institute.
Visit him at edwardsri.com.

Includes a reader's guide with questions for discussion

Also available as an ebook
New releases, featured titles & more at

ImageCatholicBooks.com

IMAGE

Cover design: Nupoor Gordon
Cover photograph: © Dea / A. Dogli Orti / Getty Images
Author photograph: Brenda Kraft

U.S. $16.00 / $22.00 CAN
Religion—Christianity—Catholic
ISBN 978-0-385-34805-8

51600

9 780385 348058